Beyond Referrals

How to Use the
Perpetual Revenue System™
to Convert Referrals into High-Value Clients

BILL CATES

New York   Chicago   San Francisco   Lisbon   London   Madrid   Mexico City
Milan   New Delhi   San Juan   Seoul   Singapore   Sydney   Toronto

1 2 3 4 5 6 7 8 9 10   QFR/QFR   1 8 7 6 5 4 3

ISBN   978-0-07-179166-3
MHID   0-07-179166-3

e-ISBN   978-0-07-179167-0
e-MHID   0-07-179167-1

Library of Congress Cataloging-in-Publication Data
Cates, W. R. (William R.)
  Beyond referrals: how to use the perpetual revenue system to convert referrals into high-value clients / by Bill Cates.
    pages cm
  ISBN-13: 978-0-07-179166-3 (alk. paper)
  ISBN-10: 0-07-179166-3 (alk. paper)
  1. Business referrals. I. Title.
  HF5438.25.C3657 2013
  658.8—dc23

                                                        2012047673

McGraw-Hill Education books are available at special quantity discounts to use as premiums and sales promotions or for use in corporate training programs. To contact a representative, please e-mail us at bulksales@mcgraw-hill.com.

This book is printed on acid-free paper.

The moment you permit your mind to dwell with dissatisfaction upon things as they are, you begin to lose ground. You fix attention upon the common, the poor, the squalid, and the mean—and your mind takes the form of those things. You will then transmit these forms or mental images to the formless. Thus, the common, the poor, the squalid, and the mean will come to you. To permit your mind to dwell upon the inferior is to become inferior and to surround yourself with inferior things. On the other hand, to fix your attention on the best is to surround yourself with the best and to become the best.

The grateful mind is constantly fixed upon the best. Therefore, it tends to become the best; it takes the form or character of the best and will receive the best.

—Wallace Wattles, *The Science of Getting Rich* (1910)

CONTENTS

FOREWORD

It is a real pleasure for me to write this foreword for my friend and colleague Bill Cates. Bill and I have known each other and worked together for years in the exciting business of selling and personal success. He is now the foremost authority in America on helping professionals acquire more and better clients through referrals, faster and easier than ever before, and helping companies build a thriving referral culture.

When I began selling in my early twenties, I received no training except the words "go out and talk to as many people as you can." I worked for many months, making calls and going from door to door, making very few sales, and feeling both frustrated and inadequate. Finally, I began asking the question "Why is it that some salespeople are more successful than others?" The answers changed my career and my life. Once I learned how to sell professionally, my sales increased dramatically. Soon I was recruiting and training other people with my sales ideas. By the time I was 26, I was responsible for six countries and had 95 people under my control, each one of whom I had recruited and trained personally.

Since those early days, I have developed sales training systems that have now been used in 60 countries to train more than 2 million salespeople. Many of the graduates of my programs have gone on to lead their fields, become the top income earners in their professions, own their own businesses, and become self-made millionaires.

One of the factors I discovered was that top salespeople were *professionals*. They understood every part of the selling process, and they followed a definite plan and schedule to achieve exceptional sales results.

Another key factor I discovered was that top salespeople were extremely good at getting referrals from each customer or non-customer. These referrals led them to more and better sales, faster, and easier. Eventually, the top professionals I worked with developed their careers so that they worked "by referral only."

I only wish that I had known the wonderful strategies and techniques that Bill Cates teaches in this book earlier in my career. By following these ideas, salespeople, small business owners, and professionals of all types can create more referrals and stimulate more word-of-mouth sales than they ever thought possible.

It turns out that the highest-paid salespeople in every field, and the highest-paid professionals, are all excellent at getting referrals from one client to another. And the good news is that this is a skill that you can learn, and quite quickly. If you ask properly, referrals are easy to get. Referrals cost nothing. Referrals dramatically reduce the amount of time it takes for you to get in front of a prospective client. Your closing ratio with referrals is higher. The sales process is faster. A good referral will lead you to other referrals from the customer's personal and business circle. Referrals are truly the "keys to the kingdom" of sales success and high income.

This book will help you convert the referrals you get to what Bill calls "Engaged Introductions." An engaged introduction is a collaborative effort where the referral source works with you to make sure you get connected to the new prospect. An engaged introduction is not just word of mouth. And it's not just "give her a call and feel free to use my name." An engaged introduction gets your foot in the door and establishes a genuine connection between you and the new prospect.

Bill Cates has coined the term "The Law of Perpetual Revenue" and created "The Perpetual Revenue System." This is a great concept in the field of selling. It requires that you serve your clients well. This leads to referrals. Referrals lead to introductions, which lead to appointments, which lead to new clients. And the cycle continues—*perpetually*.

There has never been another book like this. There are books on referrals. There are books on sales skills. But no one, until now, has written a book designed to help you turn referrals into new clients. When you follow the steps that Bill has explained in this book, you will be on your way to perpetual revenue. So, if you are ready for a career-changing experience, put up your tray table and do up your seat belt. Bill Cates is going to take you on a journey to the highest levels of sales and sales income possible for you in the exciting months and years ahead.

Brian Tracy, 2012

PREFACE

When I graduated from the University of Maryland (go Terps!),
I was shy, lacked confidence, and had a degree in sociology.
So, naturally, I took a job in sales. My first job was selling home
improvement services. It wasn't a very sophisticated selling situation.
In fact, we didn't even set our own appointments. They were set for us,
and we just showed up trying to make the sale.

So I was 22 and my sales manager, Larry, was 23. He had been in
the business about nine months, and so he was the "veteran" among
us. For the first three weeks, my job was to observe Larry make sales.
My fourth week on the job, I started to run the appointments and
Larry observed me.

I'll never forget my first sale. In fact, it left an indelible mark on
my consciousness. It was a nice home in Bethesda, Maryland, a
suburb of Washington, D.C. I had driven that night, and as I began to
start the car, Larry put his hands on the keys and wouldn't let me start
the car.

"What's up Larry? Do you want to debrief or something?"

"Actually, Bill. You forgot the most important thing."

"I got the contract; it's signed. And I got the check; it's signed.
What did I forget?"

"You forgot to ask for referrals."

"You're right! Tell you what. I'll call the homeowners tomorrow
and see if I can get some over the phone."

"Well, actually Bill, I was thinking it would be a good training experience for you to get out of the car now and go back in and ask for referrals."

Now I was thinking, "This guy is nuts." So we proceeded to get into an argument—my fourth week on the job—about why it was or was not a good time to go back into the home and ask for referrals. In the meantime, the downstairs light went off and the upstairs light went on. They were getting ready for bed.

Finally, Larry said to me, "Look, Bill. Here's your choice. Either you go back now and ask for referrals, or I lay on the horn, wake up the entire neighborhood, which will blow the sale, and tomorrow you could be looking for a new job."

Wow! Well, I didn't know any better and I needed the job, so I got out of the car (without Larry), rang the doorbell, and said, "Sir, I'm sorry to bother you, but my sales manager is a maniac. He said if I don't ask you for some referrals to a few of your neighbors, I could lose my job."

Now what saved me in this predicament was that this new customer of mine was a sales manager. So not only did he appreciate my asking for referrals (wishing his salespeople would do the same), but he appreciated the courage it took to go back and ask for referrals. He said, "Come on in. I'll help you out." He sat me down and proceeded to give me three great referrals. He gave me full contact information and told me a little about each person.

Three great referrals—for a new job! I contacted all three of those referrals and was offered a position from each one. I accepted one and sold moving and storage services for about a year.

Now we don't condone Larry's style of management. It was pretty heavy-handed. But Larry gave me a huge gift. He gave me the gift of awareness. After an experience like that, I don't ever forget to ask for referrals. Sometimes I decide "Now's not the right time," and I've even wimped out from time to time. But I never forget. (And I've actually built a highly successful business teaching others how to acquire more clients through referrals. How ironic is that?)

What I hope to do with this book, in a kinder, gentler way, is bring that same awareness to you. Awareness is a powerful thing. When you're aware of what's possible, you tend to see opportunities and take action. I'm hoping this book will show you the opportunity that is in front of you every day—referrals from your happy clients—and then give you the tools to leverage those referrals into introductions, appointments, and new clients. You're probably sitting on a gold mine of opportunity. Let's go capture that together.

ACKNOWLEDGMENTS

I've been fortunate to surround myself with an extremely supportive group of friends and colleagues. Either directly or indirectly, they have contributed to the success of my writing this book, as well as the success of my business.

My Staff. Jennifer Kreitzer, Jennifer Hill, and Kevin Schriver

My MasterMind group. Steven Gaffney, Willie Jolley, Marissa Levin, Suzi Pomerantz, and Zemira Jones

My men's team. John Hurley, Jay Magenheim, Les Picker, Randy Richie, and Joel Rosenberg

My support team at McGraw-Hill. Donya Dickerson, Janice Race, and Cheryl Hudson

My family. Jenna Cates, Lee Bristol, Kris Cates-Bristol, Jessica Cates-Bristol, Kate McCrae, Joe Schoenbaur, and Nancy Bierer.

INTRODUCTION

THE PERPETUAL REVENUE SYSTEM™

For 18 years, I've been helping businesses of all sizes acquire new clients through referrals. For individual sales professionals, to small business owners, to Fortune 100 companies, I've produced growth for my clients. My first three books focused on the referral process itself—becoming more referable, getting referrals without asking, asking in a confident manner without pushing or begging, networking more effectively, using reputation marketing, and engaging in all the other strategies that generate an unlimited supply of referrals. But a referral isn't the end game, is it? Getting a referral is only a means to an end in your efforts to obtain a new client. While a referral is clearly the best way to meet a prospect, your process can't stop there. Allow me to introduce you to the Perpetual Revenue System.

Satisfied clients give you referrals (sometimes without even asking). You turn those referrals into introductions so that the new prospects will be open to hearing from you. From the introduction, you set an appointment to begin the client-courtship process. From there, you endeavor to win the new clients and make the sale. As you provide great value to the new clients, the process starts all over again. It's simple. It's easy. And you can get this going right now!

One of the beautiful aspects of this dynamic is that it does not result in linear growth, one new client at a time. This process creates exponential growth, where one client can lead to two, two to four, four to eight, and so on. Your business grows geometrically!

Why Referrals Are Best

If you've picked up this book, then you probably have a sense of why you want to get more referrals. But let's make sure you know the full benefit of working from referrals.

1. Referrals cost you nothing to acquire. (Do you know your "cost per lead" with other lead-generation methods?) The only cost of a referral might be a small thank you gift.

2. You start at a higher point of trust. When you meet a new prospect for the first time, you need to show up "trustworthy." There is no better way to show up worthy of one's trust than through an introduction from someone the prospect already trusts. Referrals are "borrowed trust." You

borrow the trust in one relationship long enough to establish your own trust in the new relationship.

3. Your price is usually less of an issue. While your price, fee, or however you charge for your products or services is never off the table, when you work from referrals, people are almost always willing to pay a little more when you've been recommended by someone they trust. (There's that word *trust* again. It's a topic we'll deal with throughout this book.) In fact, if a significant component of your client attraction plan is referrals, you can usually charge more for your products and services.

4. Your sales process moves faster. Most sales that start with a referral move through the sales process more quickly. Sales come faster because, again, you start at a higher point of trust. Many prospects come to you predisposed to do business with you.

5. Your "closing ratio" is higher. Most salespeople experience closing ratios of 10 to 30 percent from other lead sources. Referral-based sales usually close at 50 to 70 percent (sometimes even higher).

6. Your sales are often larger. *Example:* In the life insurance industry, a sale ("case size") resulting from a referral is twice as large as those that come from other sources. Work from referrals and double your income! There's a novel idea.

7. Your new prospects and clients are more likely to follow your suggestions. Prospects and clients you meet through referrals will follow your suggestions because they know their friend or colleague has had a good experience in following your recommendations.

8. Referrals beget referrals. A client obtained through a referral is more likely to give referrals. And since many clients will give you multiple referrals over time, your business growth is exponential.

9. It's a fun way to do business! You can create a "referral lifestyle" where the prospects you call want to hear from you, want to meet with you, trust you more from the start, and even call you!

Referrals Aren't Enough!

Have you noticed how crazy busy everyone seems to be these days? Have you noticed how it's hard enough to reach your clients, let alone your prospects? Have you noticed how hard it's become to cut through the noise that your prospects experience every day just to grab their attention for a minute or two? Referrals are not enough. *We have to think in terms of introductions!* When you've been introduced to a prospect, that prospect's interest is piqued; that prospect is more likely to answer your call, return your call, or reply to your e-mail.

This book will help you convert the referrals you get into *engaged introductions*. An engaged introduction is a collaborative effort where the referral source works with you to make sure you get connected to the new prospect. An engaged introduction is not just word of mouth. And it's not just "give her a call and feel free to use my name." An engaged introduction gets your foot in the door and establishes a genuine connection between you and the new prospect.

It's Different When You Work from Referrals

After you've received the referral, you have to set the appointment with the new prospect. Depending on your business model, the appointment may be in person or may take place over the phone. Contacting your prospects and setting appointments look different when you work from referrals (over other types of lead sources). What you learn about the new prospect from your referral source helps you craft a much more compelling reason for why that prospect should give you a piece of his or her valuable time.

You see, just because you've met someone through a referral, it doesn't mean that person is going to meet with you. Of course, when the trust level between the referral source and the new prospect is high, that is sometimes enough to move the sales process along. But not always. In most cases, you have to continue to deliver value and build trust so that the prospect warms up to meeting with you. This book will give you some concrete ideas, proven methods, and best practices for turning introductions into appointments.

Sales Is Not a Four-Letter Word

As previously stated, the goal of sales and marketing is gaining a new client. And "closing the sale" is not about tricky, manipulative closing techniques. In fact, I've never liked the word *closing*. That's because making the sale is not the end of the relationship or the closing of the sales process. It's the beginning. And if you trick people into buying from you, then their reaction may be regret. This can lead to cancellations and certainly no referrals. While you will see me use the word *closing* from time to time, think in terms of *confirming* the sale or *confirming* the new relationship.

Making a sale is much more than saying to your clients, "Here's what I do. Here's how well I do it. Wanna buy from me?" This is an oversimplistic picture of what's going on out there with many salespeople, small business owners, and professionals. They present their value proposition and think that's enough. Unfortunately for them, sometimes it is. This leads to laziness in the sales process.

This book will give you a model for converting a referral prospect into a new client in a way that all parties feel good about the process. When you bring on new clients in the right way, you can become highly referable very early in the new relationship. This, in turn, allows you to keep the Law of Perpetual Revenue running smoothly.

Build a Referral Culture

I often call referrals "forgotten gold." Most businesses know the importance and effectiveness of referrals and introductions, but very few have strived to build a referral-based business. They give lip service to referrals, but they rarely train their people how to generate referrals. Some companies have adopted the practice of measuring their Net Promoter Score. The Net Promoted Score is a customer loyalty metric developed by (and a registered trademark of) Fred Reichheld, Bain & Company, and Satmetrix. It measures the ratios of customers from a low range of "detractors" to a high range of "promoters." Proponents of the Net Promoter Score say that it's the most important metric in measuring customer service: will the customer promote our business to others? While this is certainly a worthwhile measurement, most companies don't go to the next step of leveraging these scores. They don't become proactive in turning promoters into connectors. They encourage word of mouth, but they don't go for referrals and introductions. Stopping at worth of mouth is an incomplete growth process. To maximize new-client growth through referrals, you have to be referable and you have to be proactive.

This Book Is Worthless

My mentor in sales, Mr. Bill Wilks, told me many times, "Billy Cates, ideas do not make you more successful. Only *acting* on ideas will lead to success." Please don't read this book and say to yourself as you read, "That's a good idea. Oh, that's a good idea too," and then do nothing about that idea. Every time you read an idea that you think you can apply to your business, put down the book and record it, share it with a colleague (could be by e-mail), or even add it to your calendar to work on later. This book is worthless unless you act on the ideas I present. The good news for you is that every single idea, strategy, and tactic in this book has been proved to work. This is not a book of philosophy; it's a book of action. Take it!

SECTION I

GET MORE REFERRALS

Leverage Your Successful Relationships

The first part of the Perpetual Revenue System is about generating referrals. There are two overarching strategies that will help you get more referrals:

1. Be more referable.

2. Be more proactive.

If you've read either of my last two books on referrals, *Get More Referrals Now!* (McGraw-Hill) or *Don't Keep Me a Secret!* (McGraw-Hill), then you already have some great ideas and strategies to help you create a steady flow of referrals. Are you acting on those ideas? (If you haven't figured it out yet, I'm going to keep harping on the fact that ideas don't make you successful. Only acting on ideas leads to success.)

If you haven't had the pleasure of reading my first two books, I have some advice. Read this book first. If you like what I have to say here, you're gonna love those books! (Shameless promotion, I know!)

John Assaraf and Murray Smith, in their book *The Answer* (Atria Books, 2008), describe the power of referrals this way: "You're no doubt familiar with the amazing power of compounding interest, which has often been called 'the Eighth Wonder of the World.' There is a similar force in business, just as powerful and in many ways more important: the power of the compounding customer. Customers who love what you do for them will tell others, who will then tell still more people. There is no marketing force more powerful than positive word of mouth from a satisfied customer. This is not news to you; everyone knows this. The question is, how do you create that positive word of mouth?"

I would take this a little further and say that word of mouth, as good as that is, isn't enough for most businesses. Certainly word of mouth can help grow a business, but most businesses need more. They need connections—referrals and introductions—to these new prospects, so that they can become proactive instead of reactive.

This first section is all about how to generate more referrals—how to become more referable and more proactive.

YOUR REFERRAL MINDSET

1

STRENGTHEN YOUR REFERRAL MINDSET

Your beliefs and awareness with regard to referrals is what will ultimately determine your success with generating referrals. If you believe something is possible, then you'll see the opportunities. Once you see the opportunities, you can apply the right strategy or tactic to produce results. On the other hand, if you do not believe something is possible, then your awareness will be shut down, along with the possibilities of taking action and producing results. Ultimately, your belief system is your foundation for all success in life—business and personal.

Applying the above concept to referrals, I call this having a *referral mindset*. This chapter will help you examine your own referral mindset—where it's strong and where you might need to work.

ELEMENTS OF YOUR REFERRAL MINDSET

There are many qualities that go into a powerful referral mindset. Here are the top five:

1. **Are you committed to referrals?** Have you made the decision to build a business based on how your new clients would prefer to meet you? I don't care what industry you work in; it won't affect the way your next great client would prefer to meet you—and that is through an introduction from someone the prospect already trusts. Are you dabbling in referrals, knowing what to do with one when you trip over it? Or have you made a commitment to referrals? How do you know? Look at your actions, not your intentions. The way of the world is meeting people through other people, and the referral is the warm way we get into their lives.

2. **Do you believe asking for referrals is safe?** I've been teaching my referral system since 1996, and one thing is very clear to me. Most people are afraid to ask for referrals. They don't see asking for referrals as a safe thing to do. If you believe that asking for referrals is risky, guess what? You won't even see the opportunities that are right in front of you. This is a limiting belief that shuts down your awareness, actions, and results. Never fear, Chapter 4 will show you that there are ways to ask for referrals that aren't pushy and don't come across as begging. You'll see that being proactive for referrals is a very safe thing to do. Then this limiting belief will be transformed into an expansive belief.

3. **Are you giving referrals?** Finish this sentence for me: "As you give you _____." Receive! It works in all aspects of our lives, including the referral process. One of the fastest ways to start getting referrals is to start giving referrals—to your prospects, your clients, your colleagues, your friends, and your family. Just start playing the *giving game*, and you will see how it comes back to you. If you are reluctant to give referrals, how can you expect to create a culture of referrals within your business where clients are giving referrals to you?

4. **Do you have a process to generate referrals?** Most people see referrals as a bonus for doing a good job with their clients. They don't have any processes in place to make sure they are

leveraging their hard work. Generating referrals is not just about serving your clients well, though that's important. To get more referrals that turn into clients, you have to be more referable, and you have to be more proactive. You can wish and hope for referrals. Not a good plan. Or you can adopt a few processes that start generating referrals right away. That's what this book is all about.

5. **Do you expect referrals?** Would you agree that going into any particular situation expecting a certain result increases the chances to achieve that result? Of course it does. It doesn't guarantee it, but it increases the chances. Enter every new relationship with *confident awareness*. You are confident in the work you do and how you help your prospects and clients. And you are aware of all the connections in their lives. You look for those connections with genuine curiosity, because at some point you may be a great resource for them. I do not recommend you tell your prospects and clients that you "expect referrals" from them. That can actually hurt your chances for referrals. Just enter every new relationship with an expectation of confident awareness. With your confident awareness, you'll see the connections in your prospects' and clients' lives. This book will give you the tools to step into those connections.

PREFERRED STATUS

Michael Vickers, in his book *Becoming Preferred: How to Outsell Your Competition* (Summit Press; see http://www.MichaelVickers .com), says, "All of us as service or product providers seek to achieve Preferred Status with our customers and clients." There are three levels of preferred status.

Loyalty
Vickers makes the case that loyal or satisfied customers are simply not enough. He says that, for instance, if customers are loyal to

you on your price, they can be lured away by a lower price elsewhere. While we all want satisfied and loyal customers, there are higher levels to achieve.

Advocacy

On this level, your customers have become advocates for you. They are talking about you to others. Word of mouth is a form of referral. Vickers says, "As sales and service organizations we should be continually striving to move our customers from loyalty to advocacy."

Insistence

Insistence is advocacy on steroids. Not only are your clients talking about you to others, but they have become evangelical about you. Vickers says, "Companies that enjoy this level of status with their customers enjoy high profit margins and have real market security." How do you go from one level to the next and create clients who advocate and insist for you? You go the extra mile in everything you do. You distinguish yourself through the value you provide and the relationships you establish. Many companies talk about "great service" or creating an "extraordinary client experience," but few actually deliver. How about you?

BORROWED TRUST

People don't do business with us—or give us referrals—until they trust us. Therefore, we want to meet all our new prospects starting at the highest point of trust. That's a referral (or introduction). Borrowed trust! We borrow the trust in one relationship long enough to earn our own trust in the new relationship.

I was delivering a seminar in Philadelphia. In the audience was an experienced, successful financial advisor named Steve Perlman. Steve had heard me speak a few times before. Steve has a great referral mindset and even shared with me (and which I am now sharing with you) a couple of diagrams that show why it's always better to meet prospects through introductions. The diagrams depict the relationship between the *four T's of referrals:* tension, trust, time, and transaction.

The diagram below illustrates that when you don't meet your prospects through referrals, at the beginning of the relationship trust is low and tension is high. The lower the trust and the higher the tension, the longer it takes for a transaction (T) to become possible.

The 4 T's of Referrals

Tension, Trust, Time, Transaction

Nonreferral prospects start with higher tension and lower trust. The transaction takes longer to attain.

Source: Steve Perlman

The diagram that follows shows that when you meet a prospect through an introduction from someone the prospect already trusts, initial trust is much higher and tension is lower. Therefore, the opportunity to do business comes much sooner in the new relationship.

My first sales trainer was a man named Dave Sandler, founder of the Sandler Sales Institute. Dave once told me, "Going into a meeting with a prospect based on a referral is like walking in with a bag of trust over your shoulder."

Have you made a commitment to meeting your prospects the way they want to meet you?

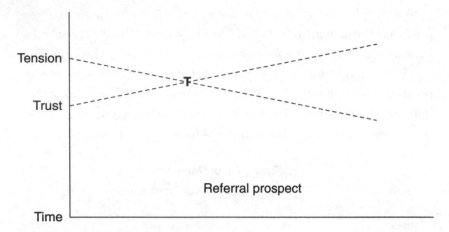

Referral prospects start with lower tension and higher trust. The transaction takes less time to attain.

Source: Steve Perlman

CLEAR INTENTIONS PRODUCE CLEAR RESULTS

A wise man once said to me, "Clear intentions produce clear results. Vague intentions produce vague results." When we're clear about something, we stand a much better chance of getting exactly what we want. A clearer target creates better, more precise decision making and action taking.

Are you crystal clear on whom you want to attract into your business? Are you crystal clear on whom you *don't* want to attract into your business? If you're going to become more proactive for referrals, you better be clear.

First, you want to be able to communicate to your referral sources which kinds of clients you serve best. Second, you don't want to get stuck taking on clients who aren't your ideal fit. When you take on clients that aren't taking you in the direction you want to go, you don't have time to find and serve the clients who do.

If someone isn't a perfect fit for your business, then you are the wrong person to be serving that person. You must always strive to create win-win scenarios.

What stops some people from attracting the right type of referral client is that they just haven't taken the time to think this through or to revisit this from time to time. For others, it's a deeper issue of belief. Do you not only know whom you want to attract, but also believe you can find those people and serve them? Napoleon Hill, in his classic book *Think and Grow Rich,* writes, "What the mind can conceive and believe, it can achieve." Vision without belief usually isn't enough.

ENHANCE YOUR REFERABILITY

2

ARE YOU REFERABLE?

Are you referable? How do you know? One barometer of your referability is that you're getting referrals without asking for them. Are you? Do you have such a good initial process with new prospects and clients that they are thinking of people to refer you to before you even do much work for them? And as you work with your clients, do some of them continue to pass your name along and connect you with people? This is one measure of your referability. And this counts, by the way. Getting referrals without asking for them is a testimony to your good work.

This section will give you a few ideas on how to become even more referable—to be purposeful in enhancing your referability—so that you get more referrals without asking for them, and so that when you do ask, you'll have people receptive to your request.

A REFERABILITY CHECKLIST

Alan Weiss, in his book *Million Dollar Referrals* (McGraw-Hill), provides this list of qualities that contribute to one's referability. Measure this against your current client relationships.

- **Trust.** Do you live up to your promises and claims?

- **Value.** Do you demonstrably improve the client's condition?

- **Responsiveness.** Are you accessible, and do you respond rapidly?

- **Credibility.** Does the client feel it's impressive to be partnering with you?

- **Reciprocity.** Do you recommend people to the client where appropriate?

- **Professionalism.** Are you on time and on deadline?

- **Innovation.** Are you leading edge, state of the art?

- **Reputation.** Are you seen by others as being the best of the best?

Weiss notes, "The more you create and maintain breakthrough relationships, the more you will receive unsolicited referrals from your clients."

ACTION STEP

Think long and hard—on your own or with your staff. Are you fostering these qualities as best you can?

THINK PROCESS, NOT PRODUCTS

If you'd like to get referrals sooner in your relationships, then you need to think *process* over *products*. Selling a product will make you some money, but it's unlikely to make you referable and create word of mouth unless you have a process designed to deliver value every step along the way.

Do you have a clearly defined process through which you put most of your new clients? Is your process educational? Do you ask questions that get your prospects thinking in ways they haven't thought before? Do you discuss expectations? Do you question their assumptions? Do you remain consistent with your process, or do you wing it?

One Barometer of a Great Process

As I've already mentioned, one way to measure how good your initial process is, is by the number of unsolicited referrals it creates. If your initial process is not creating referrals without your asking for them, then something could be missing. Perhaps you're not creating value quickly enough to prompt your prospects to tell others about you.

Leveraging Your Process

Here are five steps that will ensure you get the most out of your process—to help you make your clients happy and to generate referrals and introductions:

1. Have a clearly defined, client-centered process that makes your prospects go "Wow! More than I expected."

2. Name your process. When you name your process, it becomes yours. No one else has your process. Clients can only get this process from you. This is a way to distinguish yourself in a crowded marketplace.

3. Illustrate your process with graphic design—on paper. This brings your process to life. It helps you explain your process to your clients and centers of influence (COIs). And most people learn and remember better visually.

4. Communicate to prospects, clients, and COIs why and how your process is beneficial. Get in the habit of talking about your process on a regular basis. And always talk about it in terms of the benefits. No one really cares that you have a process; what they really care about is what the process does.

5. Bring your process to life with stories, anecdotes, and case studies. Stories engage the emotional side of the brain—which is where all buying decisions are made.

To borrow a term from *Star Trek*, your "prime directive" for every appointment with prospects is to bring value. When you lead with value, two things happen: (1) you make more sales, and (2) you do so in a way that makes you referable sooner. Never wing it when it comes to client interaction. Have processes in place, and have them documented by checklists. Then respect the checklists!

ACTION STEP

Set aside about an hour or so (with your staff, if you have staff) and think through the different types of meetings and processes you have with your clients. Then create a checklist for each one to make sure your processes bring as much value as possible; do this consistently with all prospects and clients. Review and enhance this at least once per year.

BECOME REFERABLE EARLY IN THE RELATIONSHIP

Helping people get started with your product or service as quickly as possible will help you create word of mouth and referrals quickly in your new client relationships. In his book *The Referral Engine* (Portfolio), author John Jantsch (http://www.DuctTapeMarketing.com) discusses the concept of providing your clients with an "owner's manual." Jantsch advises, "Create a getting-started guide for your product, company, or service. Create a series of how-to videos, or an automated email series providing lessons and tips, or a follow-up phone consultation. With a number of our referral tools, we have built-in follow-up programs. Driven by the technology of auto-responders, people who invest in our referral tools continue to get help from us long after their purchase.

"The point is, the faster someone implements your product or service and, therefore, sees results, the more likely they will talk about you to others. What's more, if you've done a good job educating your clients that word of mouth and referrals are appreciated, they'll be happy to spread your good word."

APPRECIATION MARKETING

In their book *Appreciation Marketing* (http://www.Appreciation Marketing.com), Tommy Wyatt and Curtis Lewsey introduce a great concept that will enhance your referability: "In today's fast-paced, electronic world, that once handwritten 'nice to meet you' greeting card has been replaced by a robotic e-mail or text message. That once heartfelt 'Happy Birthday' phone call is now left on the answering machine. Everything is done faster, faster, and faster than ever before and it has to. It's the new millennium. Alas, all this wonderful technology that was supposed to open the door to new horizons and make your business life easier has instead double-crossed you."

Appreciation marketing—building better and stronger relationships with your inner circle and your client base—is more important today than ever before. Not only is it fundamentally wise, but where your present and future success is concerned, it's essential.

For instance, saying thank you to clients for their business and for their referrals is critical to client loyalty in your referability. Wyatt and Lewsey write, "The truth is, NOT saying thank you does more damage than actually SAYING thank you does good. If you have to contact someone regarding business, then contact them regarding business. Don't try to disguise your business efforts as appreciation. They're not the same thing. By the same token, if you are contacting someone as an act of appreciation, then make it 100% about that. Remember, if you practice Appreciation Marketing principles, the people you are appreciating already know what you do for a living. You don't need to suggest it to them. If you are genuine, you are already on their mind in a positive way."

ACTION STEP

Have you implemented an appreciation marketing strategy into your business? Are you and everyone who works with you in the habit of sending out thank you cards and, when appropriate, thank you gifts to clients and other strategic alliances? Create a systematic approach to saying thank you. I use a service called SendOutCards. You can test the service by sending yourself or a colleague a sample card (I'll pick up the cost). If you like the service, you can sign up for free and just pay as you go. It's very easy. Go to http://www.SendOutCards.com/billcates.

ARE YOU SENDING THE WRONG MESSAGES?

Too often, small business owners, salespeople, and professionals unknowingly send signals to their clients that negate their desire for more referrals.

I'm Too Busy

Be careful about sending the "I'm-too-busy-to-take-on-new-clients" message. When your clients have trouble reaching you or you always appear overwhelmed to them, consciously or unconsciously they are thinking, "She's far too busy for me to refer my colleagues to her." Make sure every customer-facing person in your organization gets this message too. Several years ago, I was considering hiring a vendor to help with a project. I heard him deliver a seminar that made me change my mind. Several times during the session he talked about how busy he was, how busy all his people were, how he had to be careful about taking on more business. In an effort to "impress" the audience about how successful he was, he was actually turning business away.

See How Successful I Am?

If your business is the type that deals with very successful people, you can easily fall into this trap. We know that successful people like to deal with other successful people. So we choose clothing, vehicles, and timepieces that radiate success. However, in this dynamic, we can give the impression that perhaps we are so successful that we don't need any new clients.

Now, there's nothing wrong making a "successful" impression through the way we dress, drive, and keep time. In fact, I think it's important to dress and act as if we're peers of the buyer, not merely a vendor. But if we do that, we need to counterbalance that message by promoting referrals and asking for referrals.

I've had many seminar and Referral Boot Camp attendees tell me that when they went back to their clients to be proactive for referrals, their clients said, "I didn't realize you were taking on new clients." Ouch!

YOUR CLIENT-SERVICE PROMISE

Do you have a client-service model or client-service plan? Do you know how often and for what reasons you'll be in touch with your clients? Or do you have a reactive business model? Let me tell you a little story from the world of financial planning.

Jay is a financial advisor in New Jersey. He was meeting with a referral prospect in his office, describing what he calls his "client-service promise." About halfway through the conversation, Jay told me that his prospect's jaw dropped and he said, "Wait a second, Jay. You mean to tell me this is the way you've been staying in touch with my friend Rick for the last five years?" Jay confirmed that. Then the prospect said, "You know, the only time I talk to my advisor is when

I call him!" Two weeks later this prospect became a client and moved $3 million into Jay's business.

In the financial advisory world, it's hard to believe that an advisor seemed to ignore a $3 million client. What was at work here? Probably the advisor was running a "reactive practice." Big mistake!

Jay told me that having a client-service model does three things: (1) it creates incredible client loyalty, (2) it creates great referability (Jay has a 100 percent referral-based business), and (3) it allows you to distinguish yourself from the competition. Jay said, "Whenever I start to talk about my client-service promise, I can feel the energy in the room change—in a positive way toward me. Because most advisors don't have or follow a client-service plan."

Think about your best clients for a minute. Do you think your clients can tell the difference if you have a model that drives your behavior when it comes to staying in touch with them or if you wing it with them? You bet they can!

By the way, I like the term Jay uses, *client-service promise*. Inherent in the word *promise* is the word *commitment*. I think it's a powerful way to bring up your model or plan.

The two main components of a client-service promise are:

1. Keep adding value
2. Build business friendships

Keep Adding Value

There are many ways that different types of businesses can keep adding value to their client relationships. One thing I advise most businesses to do is to hold client review meetings. Most financial professionals have these built into their models. Most other businesses don't, and that's a shame. What do you think would happen in your client relationships if you sat down with your clients—let's say at least once per year—and reviewed your relationship? What impact would it have on your relationships if you made sure the communication was working well, if you made sure the client was seeing the value in working with you, and if you brought some new ideas or teachings to the relationship? This simple strategy will increase your client loyalty and enhance your referability.

ALL THINGS NOT BEING EQUAL

Maybe you've heard the expression "All things being equal, people do business with their business friends." And beyond that, I think "All things being *not so equal*," people *still* do business with their business friends. Creating business friendships with your clients shields them against the competition and makes you highly referable.

By "business friend," I mean a relationship where you and your client get to know each other beyond the core business reason that brought you together. Here are a few ideas to consider adding to your tool kit:

1. Break bread in your home or your client's home.

2. If you typically have clients come to your office, every now and then go to their space (home or office).

3. When they come to your office, after your meeting walk them to their car. Watch how the conversation changes to a more personal nature.

4. Host client appreciation events (dinner, wine and cheese tastings, chocolate appreciation parties, cooking lessons, etc.). Keep them small so you make solid connections with everyone there.

5. Support your clients' charitable endeavors by actually showing up at their events, not just writing a donation check.

6. Host celebration events. When your clients celebrate something significant (milestone birthday, wedding anniversary, promotion, new business, retirement, etc.), throw them a party. You'll create incredible loyalty and meet a lot of new people just like them.

7. Send birthday cards. This should go without saying, but this is a lost strategy. Create a simple reminder system so you're prompted a week or two before each client birthday. Send a card, send a present, or deliver a cake. I've met a number of small business owners over the years that deliver birthday cakes to some of their key clients.

PROMOTE REFERRALS   3

PROMOTE REFERRALS
AND INTRODUCTIONS

Great service is not enough! I have often heard people say, "All I have to do is serve the heck out of my clients and I'll get all the referrals I need." This is a half-truth. Exceptional products and service should be your standard and will certainly generate some referrals without asking for them. Every business should be getting unsolicited referrals. If you're not getting unsolicited referrals, then there could be something wrong with your service or client relationships.

Great service alone is not usually enough to get the full quantity and quality of referrals you'd like. Very few companies get enough unsolicited referrals to keep them thriving. And many of the unsolicited referrals may not fit your ideal client profile. To get the *quantity* and the *quality* of referral clients you would like, you have to be proactive!

This chapter is the first step in your becoming proactive for referrals. I often refer to this as "planting referral seeds." Many of the ideas that follow are things you can do early and often with prospects and clients. Sometimes these strategies yield referrals right on the spot, even though you weren't expecting that to happen.

HAVE YOU CREATED A
"CULTURE OF REFERRALS"?

Getting referrals and introductions is not *just* about asking for them, though that's an important strategy. Think in terms of creating a culture of referrals—where your clients know how to talk about you, know the kind of clients you serve the best, and create engaged introductions.

Nelson Simoes is an extremely successful financial advisor in Canada (he reached number two in production in his firm out of 5,000 in nine years) who has created a culture of referrals. From the beginning of his career, Nelson got into the habit of creating personal introductions, mostly over lunch, but occasionally over another meal or at a hockey game. When a client mentioned someone in his or her life, Nelson became genuinely curious. Once it looked like he could be a valuable resource to his client's friend, colleague, or family member, Nelson would say to his client, "I would love to meet your colleague. Can I take the two of you to lunch?"

This is how Nelson built his business. I was just in touch with Nelson—getting permission to tell his story—and this is what he told me: "Next week I'm going to lunch with a client who is bringing six other friends to introduce me. Also, I bought a cabin last year and have been hosting clients and their friends on weekends to help build my relationships with existing clients and meet new ones at the same time. My goal is to make it as easy as possible for my clients to provide personal introductions to their friends through lunches, presentations, cabin getaways, etc."

Nelson has been using personal introductions for so long, now clients call him and say, "Nelson, I have a lunch for us," meaning "Nelson, I have someone I'd like to introduce to you."

That's what I call a referral mindset and a culture of referrals. And what a fun way to do business! Have you built a culture of referrals (or should I say "introductions") in your business, or are you still just dabbling in referrals?

ARE YOUR CLIENTS
KEEPING YOU A SECRET?

Have you ever heard a client say something like, "I gave your name out to a friend the other day. I hope that's okay?" If you have, then shame on you. We all need a simple and systematic way to let our clients know—at least our "A" clients—that it's okay to not keep us a secret.

If you're familiar with my work, then you're probably already familiar with the effective little phrase I've been teaching for years: "Don't keep me a secret!" This phrase works so well, I even made it the title of my last book on referrals. If you haven't been using this fun, nonthreatening way to let your clients know that you're still open for business, then I suggest you try it a few times. You'll be surprised how well it works.

Nick is an insurance agent in Eden Prairie, Minnesota. Nick came up to me before a speech and told me: "Since I usually wimp out with asking for referrals, I thought I would just start adding the phrase 'Don't keep me a secret' on all handwritten thank you notes and saying it at the end of meetings. In just 4 weeks I have received 10 referrals, set 10 appointments, and closed 7 of them. Just by saying 'Don't keep me a secret.'"

A few weeks later, Nick sent me this success story: "Bill—I have continued to use the phrase 'Don't keep me a secret' on all of my hand-written thank you cards. Today I received a call from a new client that found out the policy he has with me is much better than the policies of the other contractors he works with. He had the HR department send out an e-mail to all independent contractors they work with about switching their Contractor's Liability Insurance to me. I just received the copy of the e-mail and the 53 names, addresses, and phone numbers of these contractors. They have even set up dates for me to bring in pizza for lunch to meet these guys. Needless to say . . . I'm not a secret anymore!"

CONDITION YOUR REFERRAL SOURCES

Erin Tamberells, founder of Executive Transformations (http://www
.ExecutiveTransformations.com), shared this great strategy with me:

"Once a year, you should explain the referral process to all your A
and B clients. This first referral conditioning component is easily introduced casually at the end of *client reviews* or other meetings. Close the
meeting with your client by saying, 'By the way, there's one last area
I'd like to discuss with you. I think it's important to take just a couple
of minutes to walk you through how I handle referrals so that you're
comfortable with that process and I can answer any questions you may
have.'

"Then simply take one minute to explain your referral process
to clients step-by-step. It literally takes about one minute to do, and
in that one minute you've accomplished several objectives. First and
foremost, you let your clients know—without asking for anything
and without putting anyone on the spot—that you want and expect
referrals.

"You're also in a position to alleviate at least two of the most
common fears that prevent clients (and others) from giving referrals.
People hesitate to give referrals for the following reasons: (1) They are
afraid you are going to hound the referral; or (2) they worry about
confidentiality issues. If these are discussed up front, you can clear the
way for more referrals when the time is right.

"Finally, you can answer whatever questions your clients may
have. These may be questions that would never have been asked if you
hadn't taken the time to explain your process. You may also want to
ask if clients have any suggestions. This can give you some valuable
insights, and it's a good way to gauge how your clients really feel
about referrals."

ACTION STEP

Make sure you are hosting yearly (if not more frequent) review
meetings with your clients to make sure the communication is

clear and fluid and the relationship is on solid ground. Then, at least once a year, follow Erin's advice and explain your referral process to them so they'll feel comfortable giving you referrals and be reminded of the possibility of referrals.

DO YOUR CLIENTS KNOW HOW TO REFER YOU?

Many clients don't give you referrals, not because you're not referable in their eyes, but because they don't know how. They don't know whom you serve the best, or perhaps they don't know how to talk about your business. You can teach them this, without being pushy or aggressive or looking needy.

The Kiss-of-Death Way to Describe Your Business

I hope you never find yourself describing your business like this: "My clients' needs are quite varied, so it's a little difficult to describe exactly what I do with my clients."

Ask Your Clients

The next few times you're sitting down with clients—choose clients with whom you have a strong and friendly relationship—ask them the following questions: "Have you ever had the occasion to talk to others about the work I do? And if so, how do you describe what I do?"

In some cases, you'll see that your clients have no clue about how to talk about you. In other cases, you'll learn from them! They'll say words or use turns of phrases that you'd never think about. You can then use these words when you talk to future prospects and COIs.

Do They Know Whom You Serve the Best?

Do your clients know who fits your business and who doesn't? Do you think that if they knew this, you'd likely get the right kind of referrals (without even having to ask for them)? The answer is yes!

When your clients know whom you serve the best and how to talk about you, you'll get more and better referrals. And more and better referrals equal more and better clients.

ACTION STEP

First, make sure you have a clear and concise way to tell your clients about whom you serve the best these days and how they can describe to others the work you do. Next, start creating opportunities with clients to talk about their concepts of what you do. Set appointments or set aside a little time at an upcoming meeting or phone appointment to do this.

A Great Idea for Branding and Referrals

Here is something you can do that will help you get more and better referrals, as well as work on how you brand yourself in the marketplace. Either during a review meeting or just taking your clients to lunch, tell them that you're doing a little work on your branding and you were hoping they could be of some assistance.

Then say to them something like, "Say you're meeting a friend for lunch and I happen to be eating at the same place and stop by for a minute just to say hello. After I leave and your friend says, 'He's a nice guy. What does he do?' What do you think you would say?"

You can follow up with several questions like, "How do you think I'm different from other people in my profession?" and "What do you like most about the work I do?"

This conversation does a few things:

1. It lets you learn how your clients talk about you. If you don't think they talk about you in a way that makes you an attractive resource to others, you can give them some other ideas.

2. It provides an opportunity for you to pick up some great words and phrases that you can use in your branding—how you talk about yourself to others—live and in your promotional material.

3. It may open the way to create a referral moment where you can either promote referrals (like "Don't keep me a secret!") or even ask for referrals.

Do you know what your clients are saying about you when you're not around? Is it helping you or hurting you? Best to find out.

ACTION STEP

Identify a dozen clients to take to breakfast, lunch, or dinner (or take for a round of golf) and do this exercise. You'll find it very enlightening and useful.

CREATING BUZZ

One way to get people talking about you (creating "buzz") is by giving your clients high-quality promotional items, items with your name or logo on them (emphasis on "high quality"). They should be able to use these items in their day-to-day activities. If the items are particularly creative and utilitarian, they can become conversations starters that create word of mouth for you. Here are a few real-world examples:

- My daughter is a student at High Point University (High Point, North Carolina). Among the many things done to create buzz for the school, High Point is offering free airport shuttle service to the two neighboring airports if, and only if, the students wear clothing with "High Point" written on it. As students travel home on breaks, they are traveling billboards for the school.

- Harry (Tysons Corner, Virginia) is a financial advisor special-izing in helping teachers save and prepare for retirement. Every time one of his teacher clients gives him a referral, he thanks the teacher with a high-quality canvas book bag from Land's End. The other teachers ask their colleague, "Where did you get that nice book bag?" The response is always, "My financial advisor gave it to me."

- Paul is a business consultant in San Francisco. Paul has seen the power of creating buzz many times over the years. Every year he creates one or two high-quality gifts that his clients will use. In the last 10 years he's given his clients high-end apparel, sturdy golf umbrellas, top-level golf balls, glass beer mugs, and other items. Because of the high-utilitarian nature of these items (and the first-rate quality), his clients use these items in their day-to-day activities. Paul raves about the word of mouth and referrals these items have created for him over the years.

LITTLE SOLDIERS

Here's a simple idea we use at Referral Coach International that I learned from Lisa Sasevich, founder of the Sales Authenticity & Success Mastermind and often referred to as the "queen of sales con-version" (http://www.LisaSasevich.com). Lisa calls this strategy "little soldiers." Every time someone orders one or more of our referral tools, we add a little something to the shipment that adds value for the client and encourages the client to tell others about us. On a 5½ × 8½ envelope, we've printed the words "Look Inside: A Special Gift for You and Your Colleagues." Inside the envelope are three audio CDs of an interview I did with people having great success with our referral system. It's done in such a way that anyone who listens to it will find it helpful. Along with the three CDs are instructions explaining that one of the CDs is for the client and the others are to share with colleagues.

ACTION STEP

What can you give to your clients that will add some value for them and encourage them to pass on to others? For instance, can you write a special report related to your product or service that will be so helpful (not promotional) that your clients will want to share it with others?

SHOULD YOU PAY TO PLAY?

I am often asked if one should pay their clients to give them referrals. My answer is always a resounding no. Say thank you with a small gift if you want, but don't tie a referral to the reward.

First, it cheapens the referral. It can even backfire. When the referral prospect learns that his or her friend or colleague is being compensated in some way for the referral, the credibility of the endorsement comes into question.

Second, it usually doesn't work very well. I'm sure there are some exceptions, but I've worked with a number of companies that have tried to create some sort of payment for referrals and have had little or no success. A home improvement contractor in Indianapolis equipped its sales force with a U.S. Savings Bond program for referrals. It was a waste of time and money.

I've worked with a property and casualty insurance company that gave its referring clients a $25 gas credit card. I can tell you that the money does not create referrals. The value that the client perceives is what makes a rep or a company referable, not a $25 gift card. The only positive in this is that, for some reps, having this sort of reward boosts their courage to bring up the topic of referrals more often. This, over a period of time, will likely increase referrals a bit—because they're bringing the subject up.

SAYING THANK YOU CAN LEAD TO MORE REFERRALS

How you say thank you for referrals can lead to more referrals. "The experience of referring a prospect to you should be a rewarding experience," notes Stephanie Bogan, president of Quantuvis Consulting. "Showing your appreciation in creative ways can leave a lasting impression." And I would add, make you more referable. "When it comes to thank you gifts," Stephanie says, "the more personal and tailored to the clients' individual tastes, the better. For instance, a round of golf may be perfect for a weekend athlete, while theater tickets might be ideal for a committed arts patron. Remember, it's more important to encourage the behavior of referring than to focus on the outcome of the referral."

Here are four things that should become firm habits for you:

1. Always thank people for giving you referrals. Don't wait for the prospect to become a client. Reward the giving. I love the service SendOutCards for this. Through its website, I send a creative paper card with delicious brownies for only about $8. It's quality, fast, and very inexpensive. I urge you to check out this service and send yourself a sample card (I'll pick up the cost of your first card). Go to http://www.SendOutCards/billcates.

2. Get your new client to thank the referral source. This is one of the most effective ways to say thank you, and yet most people never think of doing this. When Client A gives you a referral to Prospect B, you thank Client A in some small way (per list item 1 above). When Prospect B becomes Client B and goes back to Client A to say thank you for the introduction to you, what happens? It validates the introduction and you become even more referable. You can ask the new client, "When you see George next, will you thank him for this introduction? He needs to know he did a good thing here." Here's an even

more powerful way: Say to your new client, "Jennifer, I was thinking of taking George to lunch to say thank you for the introduction to you. I have a better idea. Let's both take him to lunch. I'll pick up the tab, but the thank you comes from both of us. He needs to know he did a good thing by putting us together. You up for something like that?" Wow! Talk about a powerful way to say thank you! Whom are they talking about at lunch? You! And whom else? Other people who should know you.

3. Thank your referral sources publicly, if you can. Cindy, a small business owner in Hunt Valley, Maryland, likes to thank her clients publicly. She has a monthly newsletter in which she features the "referral of the month." With the permission of her referral source and her new client, she tells the story of the connection that was made and, in many cases, the problem she was able to solve for her new referral client. She told me, "My clients like the publicity, and I've had a number of clients tell me that this simple strategy has prompted them to think of people they can send my way."

4. Go back to thank past referral givers and let them know how many people they have influenced or helped. One way to keep track of the referrals you receive is in the form of a referral family tree. You have your first-generation referral giver who leads you to one or more second-generation referral clients. These folks, in turn, lead you to more clients who are third generation in this referral lineage. As you see this build, go back to the earlier generations and let them know how they've been able to help people they don't even know, just by getting the flow of referrals started. If your business requires confidentiality, then, of course, don't reveal names.

George, I thought you might be interested to know how influential you've been. You introduced me to Linda. She in turn

introduced me to two of her colleagues. They have since intro-
duced me to several new clients. All told, I think you have helped
me help about 12 more people through the important work I
do. First, thank you for the trust you've placed in me. Second,
you need to know how many lives you've been responsible for
helping.

A great idea is to host a client appreciation event consisting of all
your clients who are part of the same referral family tree. This simple,
fun event goes a long way to help you solidify your business's referral
culture.

ASK FOR REFERRALS

4

APPROACHING CLIENTS
FOR REFERRALS

There's nothing wrong with word of mouth. Positive word of mouth can get your phone ringing. And it's great when interested and qualified prospects call you. Nothing better! The problem is, for most businesses word of mouth is not enough. Their phones are not ringing off the hook. And sometimes the people who do call are not always a good match. I believe we need to always think in terms of getting introductions to people. When you think in terms of connections— getting introduced—you no longer settle for techniques that merely stimulate word of mouth. You work to have the connections made for you. One thing I've discovered is that even when you ask for referrals and don't get them, you are creating opportunities for word of mouth and introductions down the road. There is a synergy among all the ideas in this book that will help you create a thriving referral culture for your business.

"You Can't Ask for Referrals"

I've been teaching people how to ask for referrals since 1996. Lately, I've heard a number of "sales gurus" say, "You can't ask for referrals.

No one is thinking about helping you, and no one wants to be put on the spot." I agree that you don't want to put people on the spot, but the notion that you can't ask for referrals is a bunch of hooey! The key is doing it in the right way—so you don't put people on the spot, you don't look needy or aggressive, and you create a collaborative environment around referrals.

Much of my work is with very successful financial advisors who work with multimillionaires. There's nothing more private than our personal finances, and yet thousands of financial professionals are having great success using my approach to asking for referrals. You can ask consumers for referrals. You can ask business owners and CEOs for referrals. You can ask anyone for referrals. You simply need an up-to-date approach.

This chapter will provide you with many strategies and tactics, all proved effective. You don't need to use them all to start an abundant flow of referrals. Just use a few and you'll see immediate results.

WHOM AM I GOING TO BE INTRODUCED TO TODAY?

How curious are you? Are you naturally curious? If not, it's time to develop that "muscle." From the moment you meet someone, pay attention to whom the person knows. When working with clients, pay attention to all the people in their life affected by the decisions you help the clients make. Beyond that, are they active in their community, industry association, club, or anywhere else?

This mindset of curiosity will help you see the connections that exist in your clients' lives. Once you see the connections, you can request specific introductions.

Kris, tell me more about your uncle Ernie.

Lee, tell me more about your role on the board of the directors for _____.

Jessi, in what department here at XYC Corporation did you work before you transferred here?

Always be curious and always be looking for connections. When you have the mindset of looking for connections, you see them. When you say to yourself every day, "Whom am I going to be introduced to today?" you see the connections that are right in front of you. Awareness is a powerful thing.

ACTION STEP

Find a simple way to remind yourself every day of the question, "Whom am I going to be introduced to today?" It could pop up in your computer calendar, or you could have a sticky note on your computer screen or dashboard. Empower someone in your life to ask you at the end of each day, "Whom did you get introduced to today?"

ASK AND YOU SHALL RECEIVE

I've been teaching my VIPS Method™ for asking for referrals since 1996. It's as relevant now as it was then. I cover it in more detail in my books *Get More Referrals Now!* and *Don't Keep Me a Secret!*, but if I'm going to talk about being proactive for referrals, I think it's important I review the VIPS Method in this book. This is a simple method to ask for referrals without pushing or feeling like you're begging. Does it produce referrals every time? Of course not. But it works most of the time and never hurts a relationship.

Think of the referrals you get as being the *very important people* in your business—the VIPs!

V = Value Discussion. With every face-to-face meeting with prospects and clients, check in to make sure they see the value of the meeting, your process, your products or services, and the overall relationship. The context will dictate what this sounds like. Don't be afraid of a negative response. And if there is something negative going on, you need to know about it so you can fix it or at least let the clients vent. This is not a "value telling." Don't tell them the value you've brought to them. Get them to put it in their own words. In this way, they get more in touch with the value, and you often get referrals without asking for them.

I = Treat the Request with Importance. Why do you treat the request for referrals with importance? Because you believe in the work you do. (You do, don't you?) You can treat this request with the importance it deserves in three main ways:

1. Use an agenda for every meeting so that you manage the meeting well and don't run out of time or forget. One of the agenda items will be "value discussion."

2. If you met the clients through a referral, now is the time to remind them.

3. Convey your request with confidence. Say, "I have an important question to ask you." Don't be wishy-washy or apologetic. Ask with confidence!

P = Get Permission to Brainstorm. Get buy-in for the conversation. There are times to be assumptive in the sales and referral processes, but now is not one of them. Don't assume the clients will talk referrals with you. See if they are willing to "brainstorm" or "explore." And make it a collaborative effort. Together you will think of others who should at least know about you. By getting buy-in to have this conversation, you soften your request just a bit. Now you're not pushing anyone to do anything he or she doesn't want to do. We've found that just softening the request a bit increases the number of people willing to talk referrals.

S = Suggest Names and Categories. Don't wing it with your referral conversation. (See the Red Folder System later in this chapter.) Come prepared with either some specific names of people to suggest or categories of people and businesses that you do great work for. I promise you, the more prepared you come to this conversation, the more confident you will be and the better your results. Start narrow with a specific person you want to meet, then expand it a little with categories, and then open it up more by asking the people you're meeting with if they can think of anyone else. You begin the brainstorming first and then give them a chance to come up with names.

CAREFUL ABOUT ASSUMING

In the sales and referral process, there are times when being assumptive can help you and times it can hurt you.

For instance, in the VIPS Method for asking for referrals, I strongly recommend that you *not* assume the client is ready, willing, and able to give you referrals just because you ask. Remember, P = get *permission* to brainstorm. You want to soften your request so that you get buy-in from your client. Being assumptive in this situation can hurt your efforts. It can make your client feel anxious and even defensive.

I think that being assumptive about the value you've provided or the satisfaction level of your prospect or client can also hurt your efforts to generate quality referrals. Checking in for *value recognized* with your prospects and clients will help you get referrals without even asking. And when you do ask, you're in a better position of getting them.

When you assume your prospect or client recognizes your value, then you miss two opportunities:

1. You miss an opportunity to see if anything is not quite right in the relationship. You miss an opportunity to ferret out a problem (could be a small problem capable of becoming a bigger problem). Sometimes you can fix these little problems, and sometimes you can't. But allowing your client to vent always helps the trust level in a relationship.

2. You miss an opportunity to help a prospect or client get more *in touch* with the value of the meeting, the process, and the overall relationship. When people speak out about the value they have recognized, they get more in touch with it. It becomes stronger and clear for them. This puts them in a stronger frame of mind to give referrals and introduce you to others.

ACTION STEP

Right now, start checking in with your prospects and clients at the end of each meeting to see if they found value in the meeting, your process, or the overall relationship. Let them know you'll be doing this on a regular basis to make sure that your communication is as clear and candid as possible.

SEVEN ACTION TRIGGERS THAT CREATE MORE REFERRALS

Generating more and better referrals begins with your awareness. When you are fully aware of the opportunities that occur almost daily, then you will be able to leverage those opportunities to either promote referrals or ask for referrals.

An action trigger is something your prospect or client does or says that can trigger a referral action on your part. Of course, you have to be careful to not be obnoxious about this. You may get four or five action triggers in one appointment. Clearly, you don't act on every single one.

Remain aware of the following actions triggers that can lead to referrals:

1. Brand-new prospect appreciates you contacting him or her to take care of something the prospect has been putting off.

2. Prospect appreciates your first meeting (finds it helpful).

3. Prospect makes a decision to work with you. When the prospect writes a check, take referral action (promoting referrals or asking for referrals).

4. Prospect or client mentions a friend, family member, or colleague, wondering if that person could benefit from knowing you.

5. Client thanks you for your initial process. Finds it valuable.

6. Client thanks you for being a good listener or explaining things well.

7. Client thanks you for solving a problem or going to bat for him or her.

ACTION STEP

Either on your own or with your sales team or your staff, make a list of all the places prospects and clients typically express the recognition of your value. Make a list of the things they say when they express this recognition of value to you. At subsequent meetings, take a few minutes to share some of these action triggers with your staff or colleagues. And talk about what you did to leverage these action triggers by either promoting referrals or asking for referrals.

IS THERE ONE BEST WAY
TO ASK FOR REFERRALS?

Yes and no. I think there are better ways than others. For instance, a client-centered approach seems to work much better than an advisor-centered approach. Make your request about the value of the meeting, process, or relationship.

With that said, my philosophy is, "If it's legal, ethical, and moral and produces opportunities to help others, then do it!"

Are Some Words Better Than Others?

I believe the words you use to promote referrals and ask for referrals are important. Words have power. Words get people thinking and feeling.

During our Referral Boot Camp, for instance, we spend a lot of time looking at some of the more powerful words to use in generating referrals and introductions. Sometimes a specific turn of phrase creates an aha! for someone attending the boot camp, and a whole new course of action (and results) is set in motion.

Here are some real-life, proven strategies that my clients are using to talk about referrals.

"In the past, I've alluded to my desire to reach other people with the important work I do. Given the success we're having with your situation, I thought now would be a good time to identify some folks you care about who should know about my important work."

"Over the last two meetings, I've noted five people you mentioned who may be strong candidates for the work that I do. I'd love to get your thoughts about that and, if appropriate, see if you can introduce me to them."

"Thinking about the work that I do, what three people should we consider introducing to this important work?"

"If you believe there is value in the work that I do, you will be doing your friends, family, and colleagues a favor by introducing them to me."

"As we brainstorm folks you think should know about the important work I do, let's see if we can identify some people who would take my call just because you asked them to."

"I'm looking for about 100 names. (You're kidding, right? I don't even know 100 people.) Okay, how about five?"

"I'm certain these folks would prefer to hear from you before they hear from me. What I've found works best is a personal introduction, where the three of us meet for a meal—could be lunch, dinner, or even breakfast on the way into work. Short of that, a phone call or e-mail from you urging them to take my call can work as well. Let's take a look at each of these folks and see what approach fits what person."

I also believe that the words you use will lose much of their impact and effectiveness if they don't sound natural. Be proactive in promoting and asking for referrals. And be genuine!

WHOM DO YOU ASK FOR REFERRALS?

As I explained above, you can ask for referrals when value has been given and value has been recognized. We determine these moments by paying attention to the *action triggers* and asking value-seeking questions.

If you've not been in the habit of asking for referrals, you may be lacking a little confidence and not know where to start first. Here is a flow of whom to ask first, which will get you started, build your confidence, and produce some great results along the way.

1. **Clients who love you.** Look at your client list and identify the clients who love you. Even if you bumble through your request for referrals, they'll feel sorry for you and *still* give you referrals. Start here at the path of least resistance for both you and them.

2. **Clients who have given you referrals.** You've been getting referrals without asking for them, right? (I hope so.) Go to

those people next. They already think you're referable, and they've proved their willingness to connect you with others. This is also a path of very low resistance.

3. **Clients you've met through a referral.** Clients you've met through a referral are predisposed to give you referrals. It just makes sense that if they met you through a referral, they'll be more open to the process. Not all will be ready to give you referrals on the spot, but they'll be happy to get the conversation started.

4. **Clients you want to clone.** If you start with the above three categories, you are now a lean, mean referral machine. Your confidence is strong, and your skill is practiced. Now you can begin asking your biggest best clients for referrals. I don't recommend asking these folks for referrals unless they love you or until you feel some confidence with the process.

ACTION STEP

Look at your client list to identify the above groups. Practice asking a couple of times with a colleague or staff member (or whomever you can wrangle into helping you) and start working through your list.

ASKING FOR REFERRALS
IS NOT A PUSH

Many people see the referral process as something they are *pushing* onto their clients, something they are *doing to* their clients. If you view referrals as a push, I can understand why you might not feel comfortable doing it.

I don't see a request for referrals as a push at all. I see it as a series of questions and suggestions, all coming from a belief in the work you do and with a genuine desire to help others. At no time are the clients going to feel out of control in this conversation. First, you see if they have seen the value in your work, process, or relationship. If they have, you ask for permission to brainstorm. They can say yes or no. Either response is okay. If they say yes, then you suggest a few places to explore. If it goes nowhere, you back off. And at no time do you push your clients into anything they don't want to do. In fact, you even pay attention to their nonverbal communication to see if they are beginning to feel uncomfortable but are not able or willing to tell you yet.

When you know how to get into the conversation with confidence, explore with confidence, and back off with confidence, you'll ask for referrals more often, and you'll never hurt a relationship.

Come Prepared to Ask for Referrals

Here's a referral success story from Gordon, a financial advisor. His story illustrates the important concept of coming prepared to ask for referrals—meaning knowing where you want to take the conversation. Some people call this idea "using a prompting list."

"I just had a couple of appointments with good clients that like me, and I had some success at getting referrals the easy way. Case in point: I was meeting with a successful florist. I mentioned that I was sending letters out to other florists to generate business, and my client said, 'Let's go over that list together.' He offered information on the people he knew. They went from cold to warm in 15 minutes.

"I did the same with another client in the heating and air-conditioning business. When I was having lunch with him to go over my list, his dentist's wife came over to say hello; the dentist and his wife were his clients as well. I called my own dentist and ran the other dentist's name by him. It turns out that my dentist sends him his patients for root canals. It ended up that I could approach these prospects with confidence now, which makes the call 1,000 percent easier and certainly generates more business."

I think Gordon exhibits a true referral mindset, commitment to referrals, and the courage to make them happen.

TWO GREAT TIMES TO
ASK FOR REFERRALS

Be alert to these two times to strike: when the excitement factor is high
and when that "referral moment" is there.

The Excitement Factor

I got this little idea from Valerie Cade of Calgary, Canada (author of
Bully Free at Work). Cade notes, "I ask for referrals when my clients
are excited about the work I have done or will do for them. I've had
clients get excited even before I start the work. When I sense that
excitement, I ask for referrals—and I get them!"

Not all prospects and clients "get excited" about the work you
do, but they all see the value (or at least most of them do). Are you
paying attention to when your prospects and clients see the value in
the work you do? Are you leveraging that value recognition by promoting referrals and asking for referrals?

Referral Momentum

Brian Cosby, in Flint, Michigan, told me this: "I ask for referrals right
after a client provides an unsolicited referral. Obviously these clients
already think I'm referable and are willing to give referrals. I think,
'If they're willing to give me one, they might be willing to give me a
couple more if I open up the conversation to other possibilities.'"

I think this is brilliant. First, wait until the first referral is wrapped
up—meaning you have the introduction figured out and you have the
contact information.

Then you keep going with something like, "George, thank you
for the trust you have in me and your willingness to introduce me to
your sister. I promise she'll be in good hands. I was wondering if you'd
be willing to brainstorm a little about other people who should know
about the important work I do. I have a couple of ideas to run by you,
just to see what you think." You bring up either people you already

know in their life or categories of people you know you serve well (life events or money-in-motion categories).

If they are open to the process, they'll say yes and you probably get a few more referrals. If they want to leave it at one, so be it. No harm, no foul.

ASKING FRIENDS AND FAMILY FOR REFERRALS (AND BUSINESS)

Do you have a business where friends and family can become clients or give you referrals to others? As with any other prospect or client, the key ingredient is the other person truly seeing the value you provide. And just as it does with regular prospects and clients, this often takes more than one meeting for the person to recognize your full value.

Most people don't approach friends and family for business because they don't want to hurt their existing relationship by coming on too strong. This is a valid concern, but there are some ways to approach this that can make it easy on all parties. It's all in how you bring it up. Here are a few sample conversations that might help you move into this area more confidently and effectively.

Asking for the Opportunity to Talk About Business

In these cases, it is especially important to broach the subject diplomatically.

> Laura, I've been a little reluctant to bring this up, because I don't want to do anything that might jeopardize our relationship. With that said, the way you've been describing your situation makes me think I could probably be a good resource for you. Would you be open to setting aside some time to explore this further?
>
> Laura, there's something I've been wanting to run by your for a while, but I've been a little reluctant because I'm not sure how you'd react.

(Oh? What's that?)

Well, my company is doing a lot of great work for companies like yours. I'm wondering if you might allow me to present myself as a possible resource for you and your firm.

Asking for Referrals

As I've stated several times already, before you ask anyone for referrals, you have to make sure they see your value. This is every bit as true for friends and family. Some friends and family will give you referrals because they like you and want to help you. But most won't do that until they get a good sense of your value proposition.

Marty, I think you may know some people who might benefit greatly from my work. And I know the only way you'd be open to introducing me is if you have a clear understanding of what it is that I do and how people benefit from working with me. Would you be open to setting aside some time where I could explain our value proposition? And if you feel good about it, then possibly open a few doors for me?

. . . So Marty, does this give you a clear picture of what we do and how we do it?

(It sure does!)

Good. Would you agree that, for the right people, the work I do is pretty important?

(Absolutely!)

Nice! I'm wondering if we might do a little brainstorming to see if we can identify some folks who you think should be aware of my value. I have a few ideas I'd like to suggest. Then, perhaps, you'd feel comfortable putting in a good word for me. Are you open to this?

ARE REFERRAL OBJECTIONS STOPPING YOU?

At our Referral Boot Camps, we spend a lot of time dealing with referral objections. Many folks don't ask for referrals because they lack the confidence in dealing with the many ways clients express their reluctance to have a referral conversation. In the same way that asking for referrals is all about your confidence, so too is dealing with referral objections.

The most important ingredient in gaining skill and confidence with referral objections is your willingness to *explore* the objections. Rather than fear or be intimidated by possible objections, realize that they're part of the process and that your job is to understand them. (This is true with any kind of objection.)

When you seek to understand people's concern or reluctance, you begin to realize there is nothing to fear. Sometimes you can point out a different perspective; sometimes you can't.

Once you realize that there is no reason to be intimidated by clients' concerns about talking referrals with you, then you'll ask more often and with more confidence. This, in turn, will yield better results.

While it's good to have a positive expectation for referrals, you should never be surprised by objections. Don't let them throw you. Be ready for them—ready to explore to understand. And be ready to reframe people's thinking if they have a mistaken assumption about your referral process.

ACTION STEP

Brainstorm all the objections you might get when asking for referrals. Then think through how you'd explore each objection.

Example: "I don't give referrals."

"That's fine. I know some people don't. Tell me more. Have you had a bad experience?"

Do this for the most prevalent objections you get, and you'll never again fear referral objections.

THE RED FOLDER SYSTEM

Prepare for asking for referrals. Don't wing it! Here's an idea I got from Ben Rischall, a financial advisor in Minnesota.

Get yourself a box of red file folders (one for each client you intend to ask for referrals). The red folder makes it very visible, so you don't forget to ask when you're on an appointment. On a weekly basis, review your upcoming appointments, create an agenda, and prepare for a possible request for referrals.

For the clients you are meeting that week, create a "prompting list" for things like the names of people the clients have mentioned in the past; categories of people you serve the best; and memory joggers like family, friends, civic groups, target markets, and LinkedIn. (Every business will be a little different. The point is to think through this and come prepared with specific individuals and categories of people you serve well.) Doing the preparation will give you more confidence and avoid the referral objection, "I can't think of anyone."

This preparation takes a little time. Ben's wife assists him in his business, and so she helps with this. You might delegate some of this work to a sales assistant or intern.

Ben told me, "You want to be proactive, and it helps to think ahead. It's all about developing the prompting list."

Kevin Schriver is a successful financial advisor, attended one of my Referral Boot Camps, and became quite good at generating referrals. Kevin uses a green folder, much like Ben's red one, for every one of his clients. He keeps his referral prompting lists in the folder to make sure they are always handy and to be sure not to show the same prompting list as he did in past meetings.

He also uses this folder for tracking the referrals each client gives to him. By keeping track in this way, no referral prospects ever fall through the cracks; and each time he asks a client for referrals, he has a record of the names the client has already provided to him. Kevin staples in each folder a sheet of paper with 40 slots for referrals (he's an optimist). He told me, "Forty referrals is a good number to receive from a client over a 10-year period." That's only four per year. It seems more reasonable when you break it down like that.

Says Kevin, "Keeping the referrals in one place like this shows you care about whom they introduce you to, and it ensures you tap into the lifetime value of each client—the business you can do with them and the people they can introduce you to."

Kevin explains, "You can have another sheet on the inside that lists your favorite Bill Cates (referral coach) sayings, lines, phrases, and reminders; like the VIPS Method for asking for referrals."

YOU CAN LEAD A HORSE
TO WATER, BUT . . .

We often give referrals to potential referral sources in the hopes that the law of reciprocity will kick in. We are often disappointed. (Financial advisors, for instance, are often frustrated with their lack of ability to get referrals from risk-averse folks like accountants and attorneys.)

If you have someone you've been sending referrals to, but nothing is coming back, try this: Schedule a meeting (maybe lunch) with the reluctant referral source to see what might be possible in the relationship. At this meeting, state the truth: "I've noticed that I've been able to provide you with some good referrals, and some of those folks have chosen to work with you. I've noticed that I've yet to receive any referrals from you. I'm wondering if you are open to discussing what's possible in terms of us becoming reciprocal sources of new business."

If the source is open to this, then the ensuing conversation needs to answer these questions:

1. What type of person is each party trying to attract—and how do you recognize that?

2. Is each party "referable" in the other's eyes? Does this potential alliance truly see the value in the work you do and trust you enough to give you referrals? (Very important!)

3. How will these connections be made? How will each person like to be connected to the new prospect?

4. How will both parties know if their expectations for the relationship are being met? What constitutes a relationship that is working? How will that be measured?

5. How often will you and the alliance get together to update each other on your respective businesses and the progress of your relationship?

Sometimes this conversation gets people over their reluctance to give referrals. Sometimes you'll discover that these people are just not the great source for referrals you thought they would be. If so, find their replacement!

MAXIMIZE YOUR CENTERS OF INFLUENCE

COIs are those folks who may never become clients of yours but have the ability to give you referrals. For instance, a natural COI for a financial advisor would be a CPA (accountant). A natural COI for a business consultant would be another noncompetitive business consultant. Every industry has its natural COIs.

Here are a few tips designed to help you grow your own personal sales force:

1. Become disciplined about doing something every week to meet new COIs or to strengthen your relationship with your

current COIs. Working a few weeks in advance, schedule one meeting (or meal) per week with a potential COI or current COI. Consistent activity in this area is critical to making this strategy pay off big time.

2. Set a goal of how many and what types of COIs you'd like to have. For example, a financial advisor wants to determine how many CPAs, attorneys, tax preparers, real estate agents, mortgage brokers, and business owners to have as part of his or her own personal sales force.

3. What's the best way to meet COIs? The answer is referrals from your clients and current COIs. You can meet these folks through networking events and the like, but direct referrals are always the most effective method.

4. Never assume you are referable in your COIs' eyes. And just because you give them referrals, doesn't mean they'll automatically give you referrals. In fact, giving referrals doesn't make you referable! When they truly trust you and understand the value you bring to others, you become referable.

5. Never assume a COI knows how to give you referrals in an effective manner. Teach COIs how you like to be connected to good prospects. If appropriate, ask them how they want you to connect prospects to them.

6. Never assume COIs know who fits your business. Teach them. Bring your potential clients to life with anecdotes, stories, and case studies.

7. Agree on how often the two of you should meet. For some very active referral resources, once per month might be appropriate. For moderately active referral resources, once per quarter is probably enough. Use list items 4, 5, and 6 above as part of your agenda. It's an ever-changing conversation as your respective businesses evolve.

8. You should also work on the *business friendship,* which means getting to know your COIs in ways that go beyond your core. The more you genuinely like each other, the more productive your relationship will become.

9. Never assume a COI relationship needs to be reciprocal in terms of referrals. Many COIs will happily give you referrals because they truly value the work you do and want others to experience your value. Sometimes that's enough. Assuming otherwise may cause you to discount the potential value of a COI. And the value you bring to your COIs can come in other forms, such as helping with their marketing plan or just being a sounding board for their ideas—personal or professional.

If I had to distill the above items in a few words, it would be:

1. Formalize your approach to meeting and nurturing COI relationships.

2. Formalize the relationships themselves.

ACTION STEP

Make a list of all the types of businesspeople who can become your COIs. With the ones you already have relationships, work on formalizing the referral part of the relationship. Then begin a systematic approach to meeting as many COIs as you can. Set a goal for perhaps 12 COIs over the next 12 months, 1 per month.

GETTING REFERRAL SOURCES TO TAKE ACTION

Have you ever had a very well connected client (or COI) who had the potential to introduce you to a lot of people but just never seemed to get around to introducing you to his or her huge network? Here are three strategies that could get the person into an action mode:

1. **Target list.** Create a "target list" of the people this person likely knows. Bring that list and go through the people one by one. Even if it's a short list, this will get the brainstorming started. Sources for this list are the people that you already know the person knows. To find people that the person knows, do a Google search and see who's mentioned along with the person, check the person's LinkedIn profile, and look for lists of people in the person's business association and the chamber of commerce.

2. **Social event.** See if your client would be willing to host a social event, or invite people to an event hosted by you, for the purpose of introductions. This event could be just for your source and his or her contacts, or it could be an event where other clients and guests are present. But be careful. You don't want a large event. Keep the events on the small side so you create quality connections. The larger the event, the thinner the connections. And make sure you have a follow-up plan in place to capitalize on the great connections you make.

3. **Attend an event.** Many of your clients are members of different types of organizations, such as industry trade associations, community service or philanthropic groups, and clubs and affinity groups. Tell your clients you'd like to learn more about their industry, group's work, etc., and see if they'll allow you to tag along as a guest. You'll be introduced to many qualified prospects.

ACTION STEP

Look through your client list. Who are your most connected clients? Can you identify some of the people they know to create a

target list or social event for the purpose of introductions? Do the
same for your potential COIs.

How to Handle a Referral Tsunami

Have you ever had people pull out their cell phone and start scrolling
through everyone they know or opening up their contact management
program right in front of you? I have! This is not a pipe dream. This
happens all the time! While conducting my Referral Boot Camp
follow-up coaching calls, we always begin with success stories. On one
such call, a participant spoke up and said he used our VIPS Method
to get 31 referrals on the spot. A second person told us she received
15 referrals at one time from a client.

Getting this many referrals in one meeting presents a couple of
challenges:

1. Is there time available to qualify these people for your
    business and to learn a few important things about your new
    prospects (so you have a good first call or initial e-mail with
    them)?

2. Will the client turn these referrals into engaged introductions
    (see the next section), or are you left calling people who have
    no idea who you are?

Here are a few things to keep in mind when receiving five or more
referrals in one sitting.

1. Introductions are always best. If you don't have time to
    qualify and learn about your prospects, schedule a follow-up
    phone call or meeting (could be over a meal) to complete
    the process in a way that gives you the maximum chance for
    success.

2. Think about "chunking" the list into groups of three to five introductions at a time. Your client can send three to five e-mail introductions (make sure the client cc's you) per day or per week until you get them all.

3. Don't ever feel like you can't go back to your referral source for more information and create a better introduction. These days, the quality of the introduction is an important part of the referral process.

"GAVE YOUR NAME OUT TO A FRIEND THE OTHER DAY"

Have you ever had someone say something like this to you: "Gave your name out to a friend the other day" or "I've been telling everyone about you"? While word of mouth is good and can sometimes turn into a prospect calling you, we know that that's not usually enough on which to grow your business. We want to be going for connections.

Here's a sample conversation that will help you the next time something like this comes up:

George, I certainly appreciate your spreading the good word about the work we do. Much appreciated. I have not heard from anyone as of yet, and quite frankly, I'm not surprised. It's not that these folks don't value your opinion. I'm sure they do. I've just learned that people often put off making changes, and for me to be able to get them thinking in terms of new solutions, I need to find a way to reach out to them, to be appropriately proactive.

Can you tell me whom you've mentioned me to lately? Maybe we can craft an approach that will feel comfortable to everyone and at least put me in a position to be a resource for these other people as I have been for you. Can we think this through?

HOW TO GET REFERRALS
FROM ORPHAN ACCOUNTS

Lorna Riley, author of 76 *Ways to Build a Straight Referral Business ASAP!* (Off-the-Chart Publications), writes, "The abandoned customer can be a gold mine for anyone willing to take on new clients." These folks are prequalified leads because they represent people who've already bought and have an interest in what you provide. There's good reason to believe that these customers will be happy to talk to you again. Call and set up a time to introduce yourself and become acquainted with their current needs.

The insurance industry calls these unassigned accounts "orphans." If you are new to your company, orphans (or abandoned customers) can be a welcome source of decent activity—at least to get your momentum going in a positive direction. Here are three steps to bringing these relationships to the point of creating referrals for you:

1. **Reengage by bringing value.** First you have to reengage them by bringing renewed value to the relationship. Be honest. Let them know that you (or your firm) are sorry you haven't been in touch as well as you'd have hoped. Then find ways to teach them new ideas, and update them on the good things going on with your firm (in a way that they see the value to them). Think "value first, sales and referrals second."

2. **Discuss value.** As you reengage, start with the value discussion of the VIPS Method as outlined earlier in this chapter. These orphaned clients need to see value in reengaging with you and your firm before they will do additional business with you or provide you with referrals.

3. **Ask for referrals.** As they experience and recognize your value, once again you are in a position to bring up referrals. One important key to success in asking for referrals is to come prepared with specific people or categories of

people (preferably both) to suggest for this brainstorming conversation. Don't make the mistake of throwing the conversation open to the whole universe. Be specific.

ACTION STEP

If you are new in your firm, take on all the orphans you can. Get good at delivering value, serve people who need serving, and make a little money along the way. Within a few years, however, you need to be self-sufficient. If you want to reach the top of your game, you want to be self-generating with new client acquisition.

USING CLIENT SURVEYS TO TRIGGER REFERRALS

Do you ever send written satisfaction surveys to your clients or customers? Consider adding this powerful question to the survey: *Would you be willing to refer us to others?*

Now, just because someone answers no to this question doesn't mean the person isn't a satisfied and loyal client. Not everyone likes to give referrals, especially in the area of financial matters where people get more private. However, once someone says yes to this question, it creates an opening for a referral conversation.

Here is a sample conversation that you can use to craft your approach to people who say they are "willing to refer":

George, thank you for taking the time to complete the survey our company sent to you last month. We count on feedback from our clients to make sure we keep our service level as high as possible. I noticed that you said yes to the question, "Would you be willing to refer our company?" When you checked that box, did you have one or more people in mind you think should know about us, or was this more of a general vote of confidence—and if someone did inquire, would you then recommend us?

Of course, if George said he did have some specific people in mind, your next step is to see if he'd be willing to create an introduction for you. You would assure him that you would be soft in your approach to them.

If this was more a general vote of confidence, then teach George how to create introductions rather than just generating word of mouth.

George, I truly appreciate your willingness to spread the good word about us when the time is right. As you do so, please see if you can create a connection such that this person is open to hearing from me. Sometimes an electronic handshake through e-mail is a great way to get started. How does that sound?

Two of the largest financial services companies in the world are my clients, and they use the willing-to-refer question. They have a high percentage of willing-to-refer clients. The advisors that follow this process as I just described have been able to tap into that goldmine. (Would you believe that some of their reps don't speak to these clients about referrals? Unbelievable!)

REACH HARD-TO-REACH
REFERRAL PROSPECTS

Here's a quick little strategy that you're going to love because it's so easy to use and so effective. I got this from a financial advisor in Virginia Beach, Virginia. He uses it with his formal networking group, but you can use it with your clients, COIs . . . anyone.

When you're asking for referrals, simply say something like, "Are there people you know who should know about the work I do, but you're not sure how to introduce them to me?" Or consider these variations:

> **Variation 1.** "As you consider who might benefit from the work I do, I want you to think about people you know would benefit, but you're just not sure how to make the introduction."

> **Variation 2.** "Over the time we've been doing business together, you've probably thought of one or more individuals who should know about me, but you weren't quite sure how to bring me up in conversation. Let's talk about those folks for a minute."

Every one of your clients knows one or more people who could benefit from knowing you. But your clients' own fear or awkwardness with referrals doesn't let them consider the referral process—unless you bring it up and make it comfortable for them. This strategy will allow you to go there, and together you can brainstorm the best way to get the introduction.

ACTION STEP

Take the above idea and write it out in your own words. How would you say this? Then start using it in your conversations with clients.

CREATE "WORD OF INTERNET"

5

CREATE "WORD OF INTERNET"

If you haven't figured this out yet, the new social media—services like Twitter, Facebook, and LinkedIn (to name only three)—is one huge word-of-mouth and referral machine.

This chapter looks at some of the basic things you should be doing with the new social media to stimulate referrals and word of mouth or "word of Internet."

Are You Easy to Find?

You never want to be your own best kept secret. When people talk about you and others go looking, are you easy to find?

1. Maintain a website. You can be assured that most of the people who hear about you will go to your website before calling you (or before you contact them). Make sure your website is maximized for SEO (search engine optimization). Unless your web designer or webmaster is an expert in SEO, hire an expert. This has become a very specialized field.

2. Write articles for as many other websites as you can with a link back to your site. These links give you a great boost in SEO. The larger the site your article is on, the more powerful that site's link to your site becomes.

3. Create a YouTube channel and post videos from time to time. YouTube is owned (at the time of this writing) by Google, which gives high rankings to YouTube videos, and so content on YouTube helps you rank high in Google searches. Write a blog that's attached to your site. When people like your blog, they will forward it to others. Having the blog attached to your site also helps you with SEO.

4. Find ways to put lots of content on your site—articles from you and from others. This will build your credibility in the eyes of your visitors as well as, you guessed it, help with SEO. If you're serious about this, look into the new field of blog curation. It's an easy way to add content and a powerful way to draw people to your site.

GET YOUR CLIENTS TO BRAG ABOUT YOU

Get your clients to brag about you on LinkedIn, Facebook, Twitter, etc. When clients show that they recognize the value in the work you do, say to them something like, "Hey! Are you active on Twitter, Facebook, or LinkedIn? I don't suppose you could spread the good word about me? Let's not keep this good thing a secret. Okay?" Of course, some clients will go for it and some won't, but I guarantee you'll get a smile.

Get a Recommendation

In addition to asking them to say nice things about you on their profiles, you can ask your clients to write a recommendation on your LinkedIn profile or Facebook fan page (and any other social media service you may be using). To make it easy for them, you can craft a little something for them to use. If you're concerned about what they might write, ask them to run it by you first.

ACTION STEP

Look at your client list. Who among them would readily tell others about you on their profiles? Who among them would be willing to write a recommendation on your profile? Start calling these people and ask for what you want. You can e-mail them, but a phone call will probably be more effective.

BLOG YOUR WAY TO REFERRALS

A high-content blog can be a great tool for creating word of mouth and referrals, as well as helping your website with SEO. When people read your blog and like what you have to say, they naturally want to share it with others and will send it either to people of like mind or to people whose thinking they want to challenge. According to Ford Saeks, president of the Prime Concepts Group, an integrated marketing company out of Wichita, Kansas (http://www.PrimeConcepts .com), two main factors go into having a blog help you with word of mouth and referrals:

1. **High content.** Whatever you write about in your blog must be worthy of sharing with others. In other words, your blog must be *referable*. It must be relevant and helpful to the readers—and their friends and colleagues. You can write in a conversational tone and make certain aspects of your blog personal, but the bottom line is that someone must learn a new perspective, idea, strategy, or tactic. It must have value. Expressing a very strong opinion, or even being controversial, can often stimulate people to share your blog with others. But don't be controversial just

for the sake of it. This will likely backfire if it's out of character for you or doesn't fit your market.

2. **Ability to share.** There are two types of links you want to have on your blog page. First are the links to your various social media profile sites (such as LinkedIn, Facebook, and YouTube). But for creating word of mouth and referrals, the more important links are what are known as *share buttons* and *like buttons*. When a reader clicks one of these buttons, it tells everyone linked to them on that site that they like the blog. This naturally encourages others to go to your blog to see why their friend or colleague likes it.

At Referral Coach, we use both a written blog and a video blog (sometimes called a vlog). A video blog is pretty much the same as a written blog, just using video. Check it out at http://www.Referral CoachTV.com.

TO LINK OR NOT TO LINK. THAT IS THE QUESTION!

Whom do you link up with on LinkedIn? (You do have a LinkedIn profile, don't you?) This is a running debate, and I'd say it depends on the nature of your business. For instance, for my business, I want as many people linked to me as possible. Every time I post a message of value, it goes to thousands of people. I build my reputation and interest in my work by providing messages of value.

Financial advisors (and other similar professionals) usually serve a narrow geographic area and are often very selective about whom they choose to work with. In this case, they should be very careful with whom they link and should manage those relationships very carefully.

The important thing is that you have a clear strategy. One thing we've done is look at our database of several thousand clients and key prospects and extend invitations to connect on LinkedIn. These connections to us do two things: (1) provide ongoing messages of value and (2) let us see the people they're connected to so that we can ask for introductions.

Using LinkedIn to Suggest Possible Referrals

One of the most common questions I get these days is, "Do you use LinkedIn to research your client connections and then suggest those connections as possible referrals?" The answer is, "It depends."

As discussed earlier, once you're connected to someone on LinkedIn, you can see their connections. The level of service you've chosen with LinkedIn will determine how deep into your clients' connections you can go. But how do you use this knowledge without clients thinking you're stalking them. I think it depends on the relationship you've established with them. The relationship (mutual trust, value, and likability) should always be the guiding light in these sorts of questions.

If you are just getting to know a client, wait. You can look at the person's LinkedIn profile, but be careful bringing that up too quickly. On the other hand, if you've established trust, value, and likability, then go for it. "George, I was looking at your LinkedIn profile and noticed you're connected with Rachel Kaplan. I have a good feeling I could be a great resource for Rachel and her business. How do you feel about introducing me to Rachel in some way?"

Contacting People Who Have Viewed Your Profile

You can also tell if someone has viewed your profile, and I don't see any problem in contacting someone who has viewed it. The key is to be soft and lead with value. Here is a possible message you might send through LinkedIn messaging. Make it fit you and your type of business, of course.

George, I noticed that you viewed my profile yesterday and just wanted to reach out and see if I can be of any service to you. I have a free report entitled "The 7 Biggest Mistakes People Make in Planning for Retirement and What to Do About Them." I'd be happy to send that to you with no obligation. Would you like the report?

Then, about a week after you send the report, you can send this message:

George. Just following up to make sure you received the report and what you thought about it. I'd like to present myself as a possible resource for you. Would you be open to setting up a brief phone call to get the conversation started?

Take the slow road and lead with value. Be a valuable resource first.

ALL A TWITTER ABOUT REFERRALS

Can Twitter help you get referrals? Of course! Remember, social media is just one big word-of-mouth and referral machine. Use it to your advantage. Kristin Andree, president of Andree Media & Consulting (http://www.AndreeMedia.com) out of Atlanta, told me this: "When I first started using Twitter, I saw little value in it aside from staying up on the latest celebrity gossip. Fast-forward a few years and, man, has my opinion and vision for this valuable business tool changed.

"When used correctly, Twitter can serve as an excellent way to cultivate new relationships, build a community, and obtain new clients. People want to feel a connection, which, in today's society, has become increasingly elusive. Many clients and prospects want to know the professionals they work with on a personal level—they want that connection. Relationship building in today's world is done both in person and online. If you are not active in both places, you will most certainly miss out."

Here are a few ideas from Kristin for leveraging Twitter:

- **Host your own tweetchats.** Tweetchats are conversations around a particular topic that are arranged in advance and occur at a specified time. The conversations include a hashtag (#) to link the tweets together in a virtual conversation. This allows participants to be active in the conversation while being educated about the topic at hand. Use the tweetchat to educate your audience. Plan the topics in advance and be sure to promote the chat to your followers. And while you would not want to derail someone else's chat, providing input in the chats of your strategic alliances and other complementary professionals could lead to interaction with new followers.
- **Be interesting.** Your goal should be to stand out in the sea of sameness. Make your content interesting. Consider piggybacking on something going on in the world and discussing the event as it relates to your work or your industry.
- **Link to your website/blog.** It's hard to convey a concept or educate a client in 140 characters or less. To bring more value and content, use a bit.ly link (a URL shortener that you will find at http://https://bitly.com) to point followers to your website, blog, or even third-party articles and resources.
- **Have a call to action.** Ensure that those seeking more information and wanting to contact you will know exactly how to do so. Create a custom Twitter profile page to showcase your firm and list your contact info, being sure to include links to your website/blog.

Says Kristin, "Twitter is a giant networking party (with several million attendees). Your goal at this party should *not* be to sell anything. Instead, seek to educate and engage your followers. It's all about being active! By providing good content, and showing your personality, the prospects who are right for you and your business will begin to engage. And when they do, be sure to keep the conversation flowing."

ACTION STEP

Spend a few minutes a day following Kristin's advice. Or do what I have done: find a staff member capable of managing this process for you. I write the tweets (usually on plane flights), and she posts them.

PUT ON YOUR BEST FACE

Kristin Andree provides seven tips to help you create a buzzworthy Facebook fan page strategy:

1. **Make your fan page stand out.** With Facebook's new timeline feature, you have an opportunity to create a unique look and feel for your business page. Take the time to select a great "cover picture," or have one custom-made that contains your logo, pictures, and a bit about your firm. Then add a "profile picture" of yourself, or your firm's logo. Use the "About" page to showcase who you work with and how you help them, while being sure to provide your contact information and a link to your website. It sounds simple; however, more than 75 percent of Facebook pages we reviewed lacked these basics.

2. **Invite people to "Like" your page.** Your social media reach is in direct proportion to the number of people following your page. The rule here—don't keep yourself a secret. Invite friends of your personal page, link to the page from your website, and provide a link in your e-mail auto-signature.

3. **Post valuable content.** We are all bombarded with millions of messages each day and have learned to tune in to the

important ones, while the rest become simply "noise." The key to avoid being tuned out is to provide content that is relevant to your followers. Understanding your followers and the information they are seeking is key. Not all content needs to be created by you; while you want to offer some original material, it is also beneficial to provide links to other articles and information. People will only visit your site if they find value in it—it's a "what have you done for me lately" world out there, so give them something current and important.

4. **Engage people.** People want to feel important—they are seeking connection. Taking the time to personally engage your audience through conversations, polls, and discussions helps your followers see you as a real person, not just a financial advisor. And with the bad rep the industry often suffers, the opportunity to become personable will set you apart. Speak in your own voice, let them get to know you, and (if allowed by your compliance department) have a real conversation.

5. **Give back.** Followers of your Facebook fan page are vitally important. After all, they hold the keys to spreading your message and amplifying your social media presence. Find creative ways to thank them for following and engaging (offer free downloads or white papers; promote their businesses; let your followers know about your charitable endeavors and encourage them to participate in kind).

6. **Let them get to know you and your firm.** Studies show that when people select a financial advisor, they focus less on the advisor's track record of returns and more on whether they like, trust, and respect that person (in addition to whether the advisor was a referral from a friend or colleague). Be real . . . be transparent . . . be authentic. Show some personality and allow followers to catch a glimpse of what you are really about: post pictures, share stories, and, above all, speak in your own voice.

7. **Promote events.** Make sure your Facebook fan page includes an "Events" page, where you showcase upcoming seminars, speaking engagements, charitable endeavors, and client events. Provide a description of the event, as well as a link to a registration page, as appropriate.

ACTION STEP

Create a Facebook editorial calendar. Start with a list of potential topics from which you can write an original post or research a compelling article. Next, determine how frequently you will update your page (consistency is key) and then map out time in your calendar to get it done. Also, if your business clients have Facebook fan pages, check them out from time to time. See what your clients are posting. Participate in their forums, if appropriate.

YOUTUBE CAN STIMULATE REFERRALS

When I asked Ford Saeks of the Prime Concepts Group if posting videos on YouTube could contribute to generating referrals, he responded with a resounding "Absolutely." He told me, "In this day and age, when someone refers you to a friend or colleague, there's a strong chance that new prospect of yours is going to do an Internet search for you. When you show up on the search engines, it gives you substance and the all-important 'social proof' that you are a professional resource that can be trusted."

I recommend you set up a YouTube channel for yourself or your business and make regular contributions. As I discussed in the previous strategy about blogs, the videos you produce must be worthy of sharing with others. YouTube makes it very easy for people to share the video they just watched. Make sure you have good audio quality on your videos. People will forgive a lower-quality picture, but they must be able to hear what you're saying. The overall quality of your videos must match how you want to be perceived in the marketplace.

A side benefit of using YouTube is that it helps with Internet searches and your website visibility. Since (as noted earlier) Google gives high rankings to YouTube videos, the videos that link to your regular website will help with higher website rankings. A couple of YouTube channels you might want to check out are http://www.YouTube.com/referralcoach and http://www.YouTube.com/primeconcepts.

ACTION STEP

Set up your YouTube channel. Submit a value-oriented video a couple of times a month. Keep the videos to three minutes or less. Teach, give good ideas, question assumptions, and create awareness. In other words, make your videos valuable to those who watch them, and they'll tell others about you.

SECTION II
GET MORE INTRODUCTIONS
Create Connections to Your New Prospects

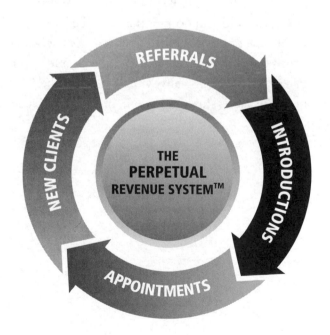

Once upon a time, we could get our clients to suggest people for us to contact; we could actually reach them on the phone and set up appointments without the clients having to get involved with an introduction. Those days have changed. With the do-not-call regulations, caller ID, and all the other ways businesspeople and consumers protect themselves from unwanted calls, it's just darned hard to reach people.

Let's go back in time for a minute . . . when there was no Internet, no e-mail, even no telephones. A person who was referred was given a letter of introduction. A person who went to another town and wanted to do business would bring a letter of introduction to help establish new contacts. That letter of introduction would be the "borrowed trust" necessary for the person to gain credibility in that new relationship.

Well, luckily we do have the Internet, with many new and creative ways to reach people. But the age-old concept of getting introduced has become more important than ever before.

This section of the book focuses on how you can create many types of introductions to your new prospects. Not every idea will fit your business model, but many will. And remember . . . ideas do not make you more successful. Only *acting* on ideas will lead to your success.

INTRODUCTION BASICS

6

TURN REFERRALS
INTO INTRODUCTIONS

I believe crafting the introduction should be a collaborative process between you and the referral source. Sometimes our referral source knows exactly what to say to a friend, family member, or colleague to put us in the most favorable light and pique the person's interest in hearing from us. Sometimes not. The right introduction can make or break the referral process, and so we can't leave it to chance.

I've seen many people, adept at *getting* referrals, have their introductions break down. I almost never call prospects without being introduced in some way first. (Almost never. Sometimes I have to just get on the phone and get the conversation going.) To my way of thinking, a referral doesn't count until it's actionable—until I know someone has heard good things about me and is expecting to hear from me.

This chapter covers the basics of securing a high-quality introduction.

SAFE AND EFFECTIVE

When the Food and Drug Administration evaluates a new drug for approval in the marketplace, the criterion it uses is this: is the drug safe and effective? This is how we need to think about introductions. We need to create "safe" introductions: The introduction needs to feel safe (comfortable) to both the client providing the introduction and the prospect receiving the introduction. And the introduction needs to be "effective"—you need to establish a quality connection with the prospect.

In fact, when turning your referrals into introductions, I think you can even use the words safe and effective with the person providing the referrals.

> *George, I appreciate your willingness to introduce me to a couple of your colleagues at work. Let's spend a minute to craft an introduction that feels safe and comfortable to you and your colleagues and creates an effective connection for all of us.*

Or:

> *George, I suspect your friends would prefer to hear from you, before they hear from me—to know why you think they should take my call. Let's come up with an introduction that is both safe and effective.* (You can substitute the word *comfortable* for *safe* if you wish.)

SECURING SAFE AND EFFECTIVE INTRODUCTIONS

Here are the basics of creating a safe and effective introduction that establishes a connection between you and your new prospect:

1. **Be assumptive.** I don't believe we should ever *assume* someone is willing to give us referrals; that's too aggressive. Once we're in the middle of a referral conversation, we *should* assume an

introduction will be created. It's almost always best for the prospect to hear from the client first.

2. **Make it collaborative.** Creating the introduction should be a joint effort between you and the referral source. You'll get the best introduction that is likely to stick. (See the section "Create Introductions That Stick" later in this chapter.)

3. **Make it about protecting the relationships.** We want an introduction that feels safe to all parties concerned. It needs to fit their relationship and personalities. Don't force a particular style onto people.

4. **Believe in your value.** If you're not used to creating engaged introductions, then you may need to summon a little courage the first few times. Make your request for referrals and the ensuing introduction all about your incredible value and desire to help others. (You do believe in the work you do, don't you?)

5. **Take your time.** Don't rush through this. Get a good introduction. If you legitimately run out of time in a meeting, finish up over the phone or over a thank you lunch.

6. **A referral doesn't count unless it's actionable!** Referrals aren't enough anymore. We need to think in terms of introductions. Once we are introduced, we can become proactive with the new prospect. Anything short of that is wishing and hoping.

THE BUILDING BLOCKS OF AN EFFECTIVE INTRODUCTION

The more tailored an introduction is, the more effective it will be—and the more likely the prospect will be eager to hear from you. Here are three important building blocks to an effective, *tailored* introduction.

1. **The initial value discussion.** When you ask for referrals, your request should be about the value of your product or service,

your process, or your relationship. (See the VIPS Method for asking for referrals in Chapter 4.) We call this having a "value discussion" with your client. When the client fully understands your value and can express that clearly, you are highly referable and it's time to ask for referrals. And the content of this value discussion is often the reason why the client should refer you and why the prospect should consider meeting with you. Pay attention to the value that is recognized. It's one of the reasons people should refer you, and it will help you in crafting a more effective introduction.

2. **What's important to the prospect?** Whether you ask for referrals or they are volunteered to you, ask your referral source, "What's going on in the referred person's life (or business) that's important to the person right now?" or "What is the person passionate about these days?" If there is any connection between what's important to this new prospect and the work that you do, make sure it becomes part of the introduction your referral source makes for you.

3. **The relationship between the referral source and the prospect.** Ask your referral source questions like, "Tell me something you like or admire about the person." "Why did you think of her, and why do you think she should know about the important work I do?" "Tell me more about how you know her." The answers to these questions can also help you and your referral source create a more tailored and effective introduction.

To get prospects to take notice of you and take time out from their busy day to talk to you, you have to have a compelling reason. The great thing about referrals is that your referral source usually has the knowledge necessary to create this compelling reason.

CREATE INTRODUCTIONS THAT STICK

During my speeches and training sessions, one common challenge that is expressed is that many introductions seem to fall through the cracks. The referral source agrees to make the introduction, but then nothing ever happens.

Here are a few bases to cover each time you are turning a referral into an introduction. Make these habits, and you'll create many more introductions that will actually go through.

1. In-person introductions are almost always the best, especially when dealing with higher-level prospects. If it fits your business, take your referral source and the prospect to breakfast, lunch, or dinner (or take them for a round of golf or to a sporting event) for a social introduction. Don't talk business unless they bring it up. Use this as an opportunity to build genuine trust and rapport before asking for a business meeting.

2. As already mentioned, make the introduction a collaborative process. During this discussion, a great thing to say is, "George, what do you think you need to say to Sandy to get her to take my call or read and respond to my e-mail?" or "How do you think Sandy will react to this introduction?" Get your referral source to think through what he or she needs to say to pique the friend's or colleague's interest. The more your referral source thinks through the introduction with you present, the more likely two things will happen: (1) you will get a better, more thoughtful, introduction, and (2) your source will feel more confident and engaged in making everything come together.

3. Always agree on a time frame for the introduction. If you can help it, never create an introduction with an open time frame. "When do you think you'll have a chance to send that e-mail

to Sandy so that I can be on the lookout for it and follow through in a timely manner?"

4. Send a reminder in the form of a thank you. Let's say it's Wednesday and your client will be speaking to the friend about you on Saturday. On Friday you should send your client the following e-mail: "George, per our conversation on Wednesday, I'm looking forward to seeing if I can be a resource for Sandy. I'll call you on Monday, as we agreed, to see how your conversation with Sandy went on Saturday." Now the client is reminded of your agreement in the form of a thank you.

Remember, you can have your favorite way of being introduced, but what often works best is what fits the relationship between the referral source and the prospect. So be flexible.

Getting the Introduction Conversation Started

Here are different ways to get this introduction conversation started:

- "How would you like to connect me to Sandy?"

- "How would you like to introduce me to Sandy?"

- "I suspect Sandy would prefer to hear from you before she hears from me. Agree?"

- "Let's talk about how you can introduce me to Sandy so that she's interested in hearing from me."

- "How do you feel about putting a good word in for me with Sandy, so she's open to taking my call?"

- "What do you think you need to say to Sandy to pique her interest in hearing from me?"

- "How Sandy learns about me can make all the difference in the world as to whether she'll take my call. Can we discuss what the introduction looks like?"

- "Here's what I've found works the best. Let's discuss what you think you need to say to Sandy to get her interested in hearing from me. Then we'll talk about the actual connection—phone, e-mail—over lunch. Can we brainstorm on this for a minute?"

- "Would you be willing to put a good word in for me with Sandy before I reach out to her? Can we discuss what I've found usually works the best?"

Three Critical Questions

When collaborating on a great introduction, think in terms of three words: *what, how,* and *when.* What do you need to say to him or her? *How* should the introduction take place (phone, e-mail, note, over lunch)? *When* can you make contact with him or her? If you always ask these three questions (in your own words, of course), you'll get a strong introduction.

KEEP THE REFERRAL SOURCE IN THE LOOP

Try as you might to secure a great introduction and then reach that prospect on the phone (or through e-mail), things don't always go as well as you'd like. What do you do when you just can't seem to reach the prospect? Or maybe you have some quick, initial communication with the prospect, but it doesn't seem to go anywhere. What do you do?

The first thing you want to do is keep your referral sources in the loop. Let them know how things are proceeding. Don't give them all the details, but if you're making progress, let them know that. If you're having trouble reaching the prospect, let them know that. While your referral sources may not have a stake in your doing business with their friend or colleague, they do want to know that you're following through on the process to its logical conclusion.

When it's time for you to reach out to the prospect, don't hesitate. Act quickly. Referrals have a short shelf life. The longer you wait to contact your referral prospect, the more likely you will be burning your referral bridge with the referral source.

Leave a voice mail for the prospect and wait about a week. If you hear nothing, leaving another voice mail or send an e-mail. Some people respond faster to e-mail than voice mail; some people prefer to hear your voice first. Using multiple approaches usually helps. If after your second message—and waiting a week—you still haven't heard anything from the prospect, get on the phone with your referral source and say something like, "Hey George. I wanted you to know where we stand with that introduction to Sandy. Over the last couple of weeks I left her a voice mail and sent her an e-mail. Certainly I don't want to be a pest. Based on your conversation with her about me and what you know about her, what do you think we should do next?" Notice I said, "What do you think *we* should do next." This should be a collaborative effort. Don't wait too long to let your referral source know you're having difficulty reaching the prospect.

The referral source may tell you to try again, or be patient, or totally back off. He or she also may offer to find out what's going on—to make sure the connection gets made. This is a very common occurrence. I have had many clients go to bat for me with their colleagues, giving them a little kick to make sure they, at least, give me a bit of their time.

SECURING EFFECTIVE INTRODUCTIONS

7

WHAT'S THE BEST WAY TO GET INTRODUCED?

Now that we've covered the basics of a good introduction, we move to talking about how to actually get connected to your prospect. Is it best to have your client call the prospect? What about an e-mail introduction? Isn't an in-person introduction the most powerful? When it comes to the method of introduction, one size does not fit all. The nature of your business and especially the nature of the relationship between the referral source and the prospect will help you determine the best way to get connected. As I mentioned in the previous chapter, creating the introduction should be a collaborative process between you and your referral source.

This chapter will cover a few best practices that I use, as well as ideas I've gleaned from many of my clients over the years.

CAN E-MAIL INTRODUCTIONS WORK FOR YOU?

While an in-person introduction is usually the most effective, sometimes your clients and prospects are too busy to make these happen. And, of course, a personal introduction doesn't fit every business model. More and more small business owners and salespeople are turning to e-mail introductions. Sometimes when talking to my clients about their referrals for me, I ask them if they'll create an "electronic handshake."

Here are the advantages to an e-mail introduction:

1. People respond more quickly to e-mails these days than voice mails.

2. Your client will likely have more courage in sending an e-mail than speaking directly to the prospect.

3. With multiple introductions, e-mails are more convenient for your referral source and therefore more likely to happen.

4. For business-to-consumer sales, when the prospect responds to your e-mail with an e-mail saying it's okay to give him or her a call at home, this phone call is legal under the do-not-call regulations.

5. You can craft a template for an e-mail introduction that you can send to your clients to make it easy for them to send.

Do e-mail introductions work every time? No. Do they work most of the time? Yes.

Sample E-mail Introductions

Do you leave clients to their own thinking and time schedule to make the electronic handshake, or do you take part in the process? Personally, to make sure I get a good introduction that sticks, I want to be involved in the process, and I want to make it as easy as possible for the referral sources so that the introduction actually happens.

There are two schools of thought about what referral sources should say in the introduction. Should they try to "sell" us to their friends or colleagues? Or should they merely encourage the prospects to take our call? I think both schools of thought are valid. It all depends on the nature of the relationship between the referral source and the prospect.

Sometimes, the relationship is a close one, and the referral source knows exactly what to say to pique the interest of the prospect. Sometimes the referral source really has no clue whatsoever. In the latter case, usually less is more.

I've found it helpful to have a few templates for e-mail introductions ready to send to referral sources, just in case they're not sure what to say or just need a nudge to keep the process moving forward. Here are a few sample e-mail introductions you can take and adapt to your business model. These are generic in nature. They will become more effective when tailored to what product or service you offer.

George, I want to introduce you to Bill Cates. Bill has opened my eyes to what's possible for me in terms of expanding my business with referrals. I've been using his strategies for about a month, and I'm getting more referrals to higher-level prospects. I've closed two sales already, and my pipeline is filling with qualified referral prospects. I've cc'd him on this e-mail. He'll be reaching out to you shortly. Take his call.

George, I want to introduce you to Bill Cates. Bill teaches a referral system that really works. I know that you are in a growth mode—wanting to acquire more new clients in a particular niche. I think you'll find Bill's strategies to be totally in sync with your goals. I've cc'd him on this e-mail. He'll be reaching out to you shortly. Take a look at his system. I think you'll like it.

George Smith, meet Bill Cates. I've been working with Bill for several months, and he's helped our firm boost sales from referrals. I won't go into details now. Call me if you like. But whatever you do, take Bill's call.

You can see that I've written these samples with an informal "voice." I think your templates should be written this way. When people are introducing you to a friend, family member, or colleague, they are not going to be writing a formal letter. In most cases, this is a quick e-mail to someone they know well. Let your client know that you've taken the liberty of crafting a pretty flattering e-mail and that it's fine for him or her to adjust it in any way that feels comfortable and genuine.

Quick Tip

When you e-mail your new referral prospect, put the name of the referral source in the subject line—preferably the first two words: "Mary Smith asked to me contact you." This will ensure your e-mail gets opened by the prospect.

ACTION STEP

Craft a couple of e-mail introduction templates. Have them ready to send to your referral source. As you're leaving a meeting where you've received one or more referrals that the source is willing to e-mail on your behalf, say, "Laura, I've put together a few templates for e-mail introductions. When I get back to the office, I'll shoot them over to you. Use them as you wish. Tweak them to fit your style or scrap them altogether. Please just make sure you cc me so I know the e-mail has gone out and I can follow up appropriately."

INTRODUCTORY TEXTS AND TWEETS

As with e-mail, make it easy for your clients to introduce you through a text or tweet. Take that e-mail you prepared in the last tip and convert it to a suggested text or tweet. As with e-mail, let your referral sources know that the wording is merely a template to get them started. They need to feel free to customize to make it perfectly natural and genuine for them. And suggest that they use an informal tone—just as they would when contacting someone they know well.

Sample Text Introduction

Our firm has been working with Bill Cates for almost a year. He has totally changed our referral culture. New client acquisition is up and so are profits. He will be calling you. Take his call! See what he might be able to do for you and your reps.

At the writing of this book, I text quite a bit. It's my primary communication tool with my college-aged daughter (can you relate?). But I have not yet gotten comfortable texting prospects or clients. Some industries (like some quarters of financial services) don't allow reps to text clients. What I do know is that more and more introductions are being made using texts. So be aware of this and be ready for it. When I know a client of mine has texted a prospect, I follow up with an e-mail or phone call (based on what the client has told me will likely work the best).

Sample Tweet Introduction

Bill Cates has helped us acquire more clients through referrals. Sales are up. Profits are up. I highly recommend him. http://bit .ly/9v3pSO

Note: There are many free websites that can take your long website URL and convert it to a much shorter URL to fit into a tweet. In the example above, I used the website https://bitly.com.

A tweet introduction can be either a mass communication a client advocate makes to all his or her followers or a personal tweet the client sends to just one person.

ACTION STEP

Go ahead. What are you waiting for? Craft a few templates and have them ready. You may have to tweak them as you use this strategy and get into conversation with your clients, but if you do some of the groundwork now, you will feel more comfortable bringing the idea of templates up when the time is right.

ATTEND EVENTS
WITH YOUR CLIENTS

One great way to get in-person introductions is to get your clients to allow you to attend events they frequent. Do they belong to an industry trade association? Are they involved in philanthropic or community service organizations? How about service clubs or clubs that revolve around a hobby (like cars, motorcycles, road biking, or model trains)?

For example, Brad is a business consultant for the dental industry. He's a motorcycle enthusiast (Harley-Davidson). At one point he learned that one of his clients was part of a group of dentists who get together on weekends to ride Harleys. He tagged along on one of the rides and hit it off with the group. Now he's an honorary member of a group that happens to be filled with perfect prospects for his business. Just hanging out with the group has led to several of these dentists becoming clients. (Yes, there are groups of dentists in almost every metropolitan area who ride Harleys together. In fact, there's even an organization that combines dental continuing education credits with Harley-Davidson cycle touring. Go figure!)

Donna is a small business consultant. One of her clients is involved in Habitat for Humanity. Out of love for the cause, she got involved too. Over the course of a year, she's worked on four weekend projects, building homes for deserving families. During those weekends, she has met a number of small business owners who have hired her for her consulting services. She never tried to sell herself to these folks. She told me, "As we work on projects together, we often work in teams of two or three. We talk a lot and really get to know each other. In some cases I've connected directly with small business owners who have hired me, and other times I've connected with folks who have referred me to business owners. I don't work for Habit for Humanity to meet prospects, and I keep a fairly low profile. But business finds me anyway."

ACTION STEP

Look through your client list. Identify the clients that you know are involved in different types of groups—business or personal. Strategize an approach to be able to go with them to one of their group's events. And don't overthink this; just start doing it.

CREATE A SPECIAL WEBSITE LANDING PAGE

An idea inspired by John Jantsch, author of *The Referral Engine*, is to create a special landing page on your website for referral prospects. This special landing page could be generic for all referral prospects or specific to each new referral prospect. If you are getting a lot of referrals, it would probably be too time consuming and not cost efficient for you to set up a new page for each prospect. If you are selling a higher-end product or service and your referrals are not as plentiful, having a landing page that says something like "Welcome George Smith! Any friend of Laura's is friend of mine!" could be quite powerful.

On this special landing page, you can offer a free report, and you can even host a special video message. I recommend you find a way to provide some immediate value to the visitor. Lead with value and then entice the person to want to hear more from you.

ACTION STEP

One simple way to accomplish this is to set up a Word Press website that will allow you or a member of your staff to create this type of welcome page with minimum effort. You can enlist the aid of a graphic artist to create your template. Then once the basic template is created, you can create similar pages in only a few minutes.

OFFER A FREE WEBINAR
FOR REFERRAL PROSPECTS

Many small business owners are using webinars as a way for their referral sources to make introductions. Your referral sources can tell their friend or colleague about your regular webinars that provide an overview of your products and services. Many of your clients will feel more comfortable with this sort of introduction (meaning they'll do it!), and many prospects would prefer a slower way to get to know what you offer and how it applies to them.

I have attended several "introductory webinars" from possible resources for my business and have found them a great way to get the relationship started. I know I'm not going to be asked to commit to anything right away. I can take my time in the decision process.

These webinars can be one to one—just you and your new prospect, or they can be small-group webinars that you host every time you have a few interested parties. You can have these webinars on your schedule—every week or every other week—for people to attend. Or you can wait for a critical mass of prospects (whatever that number would be for you) to start your next webinar.

You can also record your basic introductory webinar and post it on your website for prospects to view. There are a couple of weaknesses with these prerecorded webinars, however. First, you aren't able to answer questions that come up from the attendees. Second, if you don't really grab their attention from the start and hold their attention throughout, your prospects are more likely to drop off the webinar before you've covered everything.

There are many resources to help you host these webinars. At the time that I'm writing this book, we use GoToWebinar. Many of my clients use Webex and Adobe Connect. Some services allow you to add video—like you on a web cam; some don't. If you don't currently have a platform, talk to a few of your colleagues to see what they use. Get a referral!

EVENT MARKETING

8

TAP INTO THE POWER OF EVENT MARKETING

As I mentioned before, one of the highest forms of introduction is an in-person introduction. You can turbocharge that strategy with event marketing. Event marketing removes all the possible pressure that prospects might feel in meeting with you for the first time. At an event—especially a social event—they know they're not going to be asked to do business with you right away. They get a chance to meet you and see if they like you. Then they'll be more ready and willing to meet with you in a business setting. Often their thinking is, "My friend George likes and trusts you; I'll see if I like you first, before we talk business."

This chapter will give you the basics of event marketing as well as a few best practices that you can adapt to your world.

BENEFITS OF EVENT MARKETING

Why should you even consider event marketing? What are the benefits to you?

1. Many clients prefer this method of introduction. While many people will play the traditional game of referrals—where they contact their friend or colleague and then you follow through from there—some clients don't feel comfortable with that. Others, however, are very comfortable inviting people they know to a social or educational event. I think it's important to have as many referral tools working for you as possible. Ask for a referral straight up and ask your clients to invite people to your events.

2. You meet prospects in a low-key social atmosphere. This is good for both you and your new prospects. Many people don't want their first meeting with you to be one where they will have to decide if they want to work with you.

3. You get better initial connections. Because your events are not "sales events," but rather opportunities to have fun or learn, attendees are less guarded. They don't have to play defense to your offense. So you have the opportunity to establish much higher rapport, and even trust, before you ever sit down to talk business.

4. When you finally do sit down to talk business, you start off at a higher level of trust. This, in turn, usually means that prospects will be more forthcoming with the information you need to see if you can be of service to them. And as you begin to make recommendations, they are usually more open to your ideas.

5. When your event has a mix of clients and prospects, the prospects see the type of relationship you have with your clients (and vice versa), and they want that for themselves.

6. When clients who like you and trust you get together with other clients who like you and trust you, what's the net result? They all come away liking you and trusting you even more.

In psychology, this is called "consistency theory." The beliefs and opinions they held going in get reinforced by the event.

7. It's a fun way to do business! As we get into the different types of events you can host to facilitate these introductions, you'll realize that this is a very enjoyable way to do business. You meet new prospects in a fun environment, and the relationships build with little or no resistance.

There are five main types of events you can host that can turn into solid introductions with new prospects:

1. Social events

2. Philanthropic and community service events

3. Celebration events

4. Educational events

5. Affinity-group events

INVITING CLIENTS TO BRING GUESTS TO REFERRAL EVENTS

Imagine being able to host a nice dinner or wine and cheese tasting, where your great clients invite people just like themselves for the purpose of meeting you in an enjoyable setting. Possible? You bet it is. I've been teaching small business owners and salespeople how to do this for years. It's almost always a worthwhile investment of time and dollars.

Here are a few events I've coached people to host:

1. Nice dinner—a "chef's table" if you have the budget

2. Wine and cheese tasting

3. Chocolate tasting

4. Cooking class

5. Sporting event

6. Golf outing or lesson

7. Boat outing

8. Wii or Xbox party

9. An outing that leverages a hobby, such as fishing, hunting, or skiing

Here's how you invite your client to identify friends and colleagues to take to your event:

George, as you might imagine, many of our clients like to introduce us to people they think should know about our work. We've found that one of the best ways to make this happen is through low-key social events. I'm calling to let you know we're hosting such an event in about six weeks. It's going to be a wine and cheese tasting. We have an expert coming to walk us through some of the best wines available. We're making it a pretty small—somewhat exclusive—affair. Consider this a "hold-the-date" call. We'll be sending you a more formal invitation. Think of who you think might enjoy meeting us at such an event. And this isn't a sales pitch. We won't talk any business. It's just a way to meet people in a low-key, fun environment. We'll follow up with you in a few weeks to see if you can make it and whom you'd like to bring as a guest. How's that sound?

It's important that you emphasize two things:

1. This event is for the purpose of introductions. You want to make it crystal clear that this is different from any client appreciation events you may already be hosting.

2. There will be no sales pitch. If your clients think you'll be "pitching" their friends and colleagues, they won't participate.

SEVEN TIPS FOR MORE EFFECTIVE EVENTS

Here are some guidelines or rules of thumb for you to follow as you host different types of events to solidify client loyalty and keep your pipeline of quality prospects filled:

1. **Party with a purpose.** Be clear about your event. Is this event just for client appreciation? Or are you doing it to secure introductions? Be clear with yourself and then be clear with the people you invite.

2. **Smaller is usually better.** The main purpose of these events is *connection.* You want to create quality connections with your clients and their guests. The bigger the event, the thinner the connections and the more diminished the effectiveness. The smaller the events, the better the connections. For example, keep dinners to 8 to 10 people. That's how many people will fit around one table (and make it a round table). Wine tastings and cooking classes can be up to 16 to 18 people, because you can usually walk around. At sporting events, you'll only connect with two people, unless you're in a luxury suite or you host tailgating before or after the event. Whenever considering an event, consider the connections. Will the event facilitate or hinder good connections?

3. **Vary your events.** Different clients like different things. Not everyone drinks wine or plays golf. Host a variety of events to attract the maximum number of clients and guests.

4. **Find unique and creative venues.** Another way to ensure good attendance is to find events and venues your clients might not

be able to take advantage of themselves, such as a dinner at a museum or art opening. One way to learn about creative venues is to ask your clients. Ask them about other events they've attended. Consider hiring a special events planner, especially for the first few events you host. These professionals will help you with creative ideas to make your events memorable, as well as help you avoid some major mistakes. Claire is a small business owner who did just that. She hired a special events planner and said, "Help me find something different, fun, and memorable." The events planner helped Claire host a Wii party in the party room of an Irish pub. She had 24 people (a little big), but ended up with 5 new clients. Well worth her time and dollars.

5. **Call-mail-call invitation process.** This is a tried-and-true way to ensure better attendance at your events. Call your clients to alert them to the event. Mail them a nice invitation. Then call them to confirm their attendance and their guests. You'll always have higher attendance if you start out with a personal invitation, before mailing them an invitation. Personally, I think you should avoid *e-mail* invitations to business events. Keep e-mail invitations limited to your personal events.

6. **Maintain consistency.** If you've not been in the habit of hosting events, don't be surprised if the first few aren't as successful as you'd like. It takes time for your clients to get used to doing such events, and it takes time for you to perfect your events. Consistency is the key.

7. **Follow up in 24 to 48 hours.** This is probably the most important of these seven ideas. While the *relationship magic* might happen at the event, the results happen from the follow-up. Don't expect to see any results from your events if you don't follow up with the clients and their guests. After the event, call the clients and say something like:

George, I was about to call Dennis and Theresa to see if they'd be willing to schedule an appointment. I thought I'd check in with you first. Did they enjoy themselves last night? Anything in the conversation that would preclude me from calling them? It seems that one of their great passions is the foundation they started. I may have some ideas for them in that area. Would you agree that's their biggest interest or passion right now (aside from their children)?

CELEBRATION EVENTS

A celebration event is one in which you usually have a guest of honor—your client—and you are helping the client celebrate some milestone such as a:

1. Birthday

2. Wedding anniversary

3. Business anniversary

4. Retirement

5. New venture or product launch

For example, Joe is a successful financial advisor on Long Island (New York). When Joe's clients are getting ready to retire, he offers to throw a party for them. The client is asked to invite up to 40 guests. Joe and his team invite everyone—so everyone being invited knows that Joe (the financial advisor) is hosting this event, not a coworker, neighbor, or the spouse. Joe averages seven new clients every time he hosts such an event.

Joe didn't start with a guest list of 40. He started much smaller and then built this up over time, finding that 40 was his optimal number. I suggest you start small as well. No need to overwhelm yourself or tax your budget until you find the formula that works.

What if you had a client with a birthday coming up? Could you offer to take her and several of her colleagues to lunch to celebrate? Or suppose your client is bringing a new product or service to market. Perhaps you can help the client with a "launch party."

In all these cases, what happens is that the guests see the kind of relationship their friend or colleague has with you. This makes you a potentially attractive resource.

I was working with a group of bankers in Red Bank, New Jersey. I brought up this idea of celebration events. One of the bankers, Julie, took it to heart. The following week she took a client and two of his colleagues from work for a little birthday lunch. One of the guests became interested in Julie's work and ended up becoming a client, securing a $10 million loan for his business.

PHILANTHROPIC AND COMMUNITY SERVICE EVENTS

If you have a philanthropic or community service organization in which you are involved, you can get your clients to invite their friends to meet you, have some fun, and make a contribution to a worthy cause.

Most of the events I listed in the previous tip can be used as events to help a charity or other nonprofit endeavor. In addition, you might consider a casino night, an adopt-a-highway program, or Habitat for Humanity. I know a financial advisor, Matt, who uses his participation in renovation and fund-raising for the Boys and Girls Clubs as a way to help a worthy cause, bond with his clients, and meet new prospects. Of course, he talks no business during these events. He just does good work and gets to know his "coworkers." From this, he has "earned the right" to follow up with the participants to suggest himself as a possible resource for them.

These events can be hosted by you or by the charitable organization. Another scenario would be for you to participate in any charitable events with which your clients are involved. As you get to know your clients, learn about what community interests they have. See if you can come as a guest to their events to help them with the good work that they do. You have to be very careful not to talk too much about your business. Just be genuinely friendly and curious. Remember the expression "to be interesting, be interested." You'll almost always end up with one or two people who would be happy to accept your business-related call later. The worst-case scenario is that you help a good organization do good work in your community.

ACTION STEP

If you're not already active with philanthropic or community service organizations, pick one or two to join. Because you have to be very careful about coming on too strong with potential prospects at these events, I urge you to pick organizations whose work resonates with you. Join the organization because you feel the work it does is important and you're happy to participate even if it never turns into any business for you. In this way, you'll being doing important work and will be more disciplined about jumping potential prospects as soon as you meet them.

MAXIMIZE BUSINESS AND CHARITY EVENTS

To acquire more clients, you have to meet new people—all the time. Just like a good college sports program, your *recruiting* can never stop.

In your efforts to meet more people, you probably find yourself going to different types of events from time to time. Some people do this willingly, excited about the new people they will meet. Others go to these events begrudgingly. Do you think your attitude going in can make a difference in your results? You bet it can! Go to events openly and optimistically, and you'll meet one or more great contacts for your business. What you focus on grows stronger in your life. Focus on meeting people and creating successful relationships, then that's what will happen. Focus on being shy or pessimistic, and that's what you'll create as well.

One way to improve your attitude going in—and your results coming out—is to come prepared to meet certain individuals. With most events, you can usually get an idea, if not a full list, of all the "players" in that organization (like the board of directors or the largest donors, for example). Then, use the Internet to prepare yourself to meet these folks.

If you're a little shy at events, do what I do. Work the registration table. You meet everyone coming to the event and then feel more confident walking up to people later.

Put Google to Work

Take that list of board of directors, top donors, and the like and Google them. See what you can learn about them. Then, when you meet them at the event, you can slowly direct the conversation to things that you know are important to them or that you have in common.

Confidence

Approaching strangers—especially high-level folks—takes confidence. The more you know about them before you even meet them, the more confident you'll be, and therefore the more effective you'll be.

Follow Up

There's not much point in going to these events with an intention of meeting new people if you don't follow up with those you meet. Personally, when I'm at events, I'm always looking for a way to connect with people after the event on a more personal level. I listen to what's important to them. If I can make my first follow-up about value to them in a nonbusiness area, I always feel more confident, and it's a great next reason for contact. It's a sad fact that most people who go to events never follow up with the people they meet. Wasted time and missed opportunities!

ACTION STEP

The next time you are invited to an event of any type, see if you can find out who else will be there and try this exercise of doing a little research on some of the high-level folks. You'll see how it gets you more excited about the event and how you're able to approach these people with more confidence. And see if the organizer needs any help—at the registration table or otherwise. Then you adopt the attitude of a "host," and it's easier to approach strangers.

EDUCATIONAL EVENTS

One way to stay in touch with your clients—a way that brings ongoing value as well as lets you meet new prospects—is through educational events. The events can be totally related to the work you do or totally unrelated. For instance, financial advisors have many topics from which to choose for educational events, including retirement planning, risk management, tax-efficient investing, etc. Perhaps you have many topics related to your business as well. Whether you do or not, consider hosting other educational events that might be unrelated to your core business, such as identity theft protection, stress reduction, fitness, nutrition, wine appreciation, or chocolate appreciation.

Just as with social events, call your clients to invite them to bring one or more guests, mail them an invitation, and then follow up later with a confirmation call. If you want your event to be successful—whatever type of event you're hosting—*call* your clients! Don't make the mistake of just mailing invitations to them, hoping enough people will reply and bring a guest. You will always increase attendance and increase the chances of your clients bringing a guest if you call them as part of the invitation process.

Whom do you invite to your educational events? Certainly you want to invite your clients and their guests (and other prospects). But don't forget about your strategic partners, COIs, and even some of your vendors.

While one of the goals of your educational events is to provide value to all the attendees, another goal is to connect with as many people as possible. So think about adding some "social time" at the beginning or end of your educational event. Brian is a small business owner in Canada. He hosts four educational events each year. To make sure he connects well with the attendees, he looks for fun activities to add to his events. He uses a restaurant that has lawn bowling on the front lawn of the restaurant. He encourages his attendees to come early for a game or two. He has added chocolate tastings to the end of his events to encourage people to stick around so he can connect with them.

Always follow up with your educational event attendees. See if they have any lingering questions. Set appointments when appropriate.

Add Depth to Your Events

Here's an idea I got from a business consultant in California who uses events as part of his referral marketing efforts. Many of his events are more "facilitated discussions" than events. He teams up with "alliances" such as accountants, attorneys, and other business consultants with various specialties. Each of these folks brings four to five business owners to the event. At the event, one or more themes are presented and then discussed among all the attendees.

This consultant happens to cater to small business owners. So perhaps that's part of why these events work so well. This gentleman told me, "These small business owners—in a room with noncompetitors—really open up about their business and various challenges."

The meetings turn out to be very helpful to the attendees, and each one of the alliances who brought guests walks away with some viable prospects for their special expertise.

I think the key to making this work is that all the attendees need to have enough in common so that the discussions pertain to most of the people most of the time. This concept can work with any sort of group with enough in common.

AFFINITY-GROUP EVENTS

An affinity group is any type of organization (some are more formal than others) where people meet to share some interest or activity in common. Examples of affinity groups are:

1. Car owners clubs (Corvette, BMW, Porsche, etc.)

2. Stamp or coin collectors

3. Polo aficionados

4. Motorcycle clubs

5. Cycling (road or mountain) enthusiasts

6. Cooking groups

7. Investment clubs

I'm sure you can think of a few more right off the top of your head.

There are two main ways you can leverage these types of groups. As I mentioned earlier in this section, you can have your clients who belong to such organizations invite you to attend as their guest. In this way, you are being introduced to all the members, with your client telling them a little bit about the work you've done for him or her.

Another way to leverage these groups is to sponsor some sort of social or educational event just for them. Now you're meeting these folks in a way that you're providing some value to them in the form of fun or education—or a little of both.

TURN YOUR CLIENT PASSIONS
INTO REFERRAL EVENTS

One successful business owner recently told me, "We have a passion for helping our clients and knowing their passions as well. We are building events around the passions of our clients." Brilliant!

When your clients have a passion for something, they usually know others who share their passion. And they are usually interested in educating others about their passion. So there are at least two ways you can tap into this dynamic:

1. Cohost an event with your client (you pay for it) where the client invites other enthusiasts to go deeper in their shared interest (or maybe people would come just because your client asked them to). *Examples:* Wine tasting, golf lessons, music, chocolate, hiking, community service project, to name a few.

2. Host an event for your client and client's guests where your client with a passion is there to actually *teach* others. If the client's passion is for fly-fishing, for instance, it could be fly-fishing lessons. If the client is a high-caliber golfer, he or she can give a golf lesson. If a client has a passion for bourbon, then you could all get into a lot of trouble. (Okay, maybe not a bourbon party. But you get the idea.)

This concept also holds true for *your* passions. I know a financial advisor who is an Olympic-caliber skier. He hosts a ski event every year. And I have a client who "loves the horses." His signature event is a yearly trip to the track.

SECTION III
GET MORE APPOINTMENTS
Reach Your New Prospects and Begin the Conversation

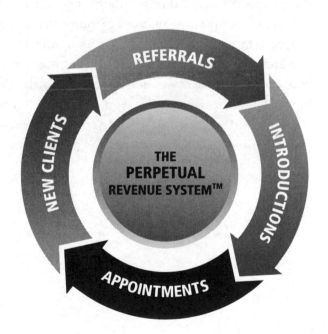

As you know, one of the main benefits of working from referrals is that every other aspect of the sales process is easier and more effective. Why? Because you're meeting prospects at a high level of trust from the very beginning. In fact, with a good introduction, the trust is there before you even contact them.

You have the referral. You've been introduced. Now you have to contact your new referral prospect. Contacting referral prospects that have been introduced is different from how you might contact prospects from a different lead source. The beauty of working from introductions is that the prospects are likely aware of who you are and why you are reaching out to them, and they have heard a few nice things about you and the work you do. Of course, the stronger the relationship between the referral source and the prospect, usually the more fluid and effective the whole process becomes.

But we're not done yet, are we? Now we need to reach out to the prospects to gain further interest and set an appointment. First appointments vary from industry to industry. Do you want to meet the prospects face-to-face? Will a phone appointment work to get you off to a great start? I rarely have face-to-face appointments with my prospects. Because I work with businesses all over the globe, 95 percent of my appointments take place over the phone or Skype.

This third section of *Beyond Referrals* addresses various attitudes, strategies, and skills related to setting appointments.

CRAFTING YOUR APPROACH

9

CRAFTING YOUR APPROACH: ARTICULATING YOUR VALUE

Before you pick up the phone to call your new prospects or shoot them an e-mail, it's a good idea to think through your approach. Do you know how to talk about what you do in a way that will create interest? Do you know what questions to ask to gain information and create even more interest? Do you know what body of evidence to prepare for this process?

In this chapter we'll walk together through some important considerations. Then we'll work on your initial contact with your referral prospect. Not only do these ideas work well in the referral environment, but they will serve you well for any type of prospecting you may be doing.

GETTING TO KNOW YOU, GETTING TO KNOW ALL ABOUT YOU

Learning as much as you can about your new referral prospects will help you in at least two ways:

1. You'll feel more confident in calling them—so you'll actually call.

2. You'll have a better first conversation with them, because you have more information from which to craft your call and generate trust and interest.

Warm Research

There are two types of research you can do on your prospects: warm research and cold research. *Warm research* is what your referral source tells you about his or her friend, family member, or colleague—your new prospect. There are things you want to learn that are specific to your business. And there are some generic questions I've found to be very helpful. I covered these in the Section II, but they bear repeating (especially if you're jumping around in the book).

1. What made you think of her? Why do you think she should know about the important work that I do?

2. Tell me more about how you know each other (if it's not fully obvious).

3. Tell me a little bit about her personality. Is she as direct as you?

4. Tell me something you like or admire (or respect) about her. (This can be a very powerful part of your opening with your new prospect.) What's going on in her business (or life) that's important to her? What is she most passionate about these days?

Cold Research

In addition to this wonderful warm research, before you make your call, it may serve you well to do some *cold research*. These days, most cold research is done via the Internet, but it need not be restricted to that. For instance, with B2B sales, you may find it helpful to call the prospect's marketing department and request a brochure (and any other sales or marketing literature). Sometimes a company's annual report can be helpful. If you're dealing with a public company, you can request one over the phone, though most companies are posting their reports on their website these days.

Other sources of cold research are company websites and LinkedIn profiles (personal and corporate). For any kind of prospect, try putting his or her name into Google, Yahoo, or other search engines to see what comes up. The more common the name, the more you need to ensure that what comes up is actually your prospect.

Regardless of your target market, you can learn enough about your new referral prospect from the referral source and other resources to have one or more effective phone calls.

ACTION STEP

When you get referrals—either unsolicited or by asking—slow down and learn as much as you can about your new prospect. Then continue with some cold research on the Internet to see what else you might learn to help you craft the most effective approach.

START WITH THE RESULTS
YOU HELP PRODUCE

Bill Whitley (http://www.BillWhitley.com), in his book *Art of the Rainmaker* (Berkeley), writes,

> It's time to replace that elevator speech with a natural conversation that makes your prospect eager to learn more about your products and services. The problem with elevator speeches is that they are too long and sound too contrived. I've often heard that a good elevator speech should last thirty seconds. When you are meeting someone for the first time (especially over the phone for your first call) thirty

seconds is an eternity when describing what you do. I think there is a much better way. I call this a *Client Attraction Conversation*. Your goal is to deliver a WOW that engages and kindles the person's interest while opening the door for you to share more in the conversation.

A good sales conversation has three basic parts:

1. What do you do? This is your WOW line.

2. What do you mean? This is your HOW line.

3. How do you do that? This is your Client Attraction Story.

Instead of telling people what you do, start with the *result* or *outcome* of what you do. For example, an accountant might say, "I help people reduce their taxes." A financial advisor might say, "I help people avoid the three biggest financial mistakes most people make." If I received an answer like that, I guarantee I would follow up with, "Wow, what are the three mistakes?" With that kind of response the person now has permission to tell his or her Client Attraction Story.

Here is a sample sales conversation between a prospect and a financial advisor who provides investment and retirement planning:

1. What do you do? (Wow Line) "I help people avoid the three biggest investment mistakes most people make."

2. What are the biggest mistakes? (How Line) "The biggest mistake is lack of diversification . . . it's the single biggest reason that people lose a lot of money they shouldn't lose. I make sure people diversify properly."

3. What do you mean? (Client Attraction Story) "One of my clients, who's in the furniture business, was not diversifying his portfolio properly . . ."

Using the Word Mistake

I just wanted to put a plug in for you using the word *mistake* in how you talk about your business. When you tell people you help them "avoid the most common mistakes," they often begin to wonder if they are making those mistakes. It creates curiosity. Sometimes it creates doubt about who they are currently using.

PILLOW TALK

Here's an idea I picked up from Lisa Sasevich (http://www .LisaSasevich.com), founder of the Sales Authenticity & Success Mastermind and, as noted earlier in the book, often referred to as the "queen of sales conversion."

When crafting the words you use to talk about the value you bring to your prospects and clients, try to avoid the mistake that most business folks make. Most businesses, salespeople, and other professionals talk in "marketing speak" or their industry jargon. Lisa contends you'll always be more effective when talking about your business using the same words your prospects already have in their head. Dirk Zeller, author of *Telephone Sales for Dummies* (John Wiley & Sons), calls this "putting on customer-colored glasses."

One example Lisa uses is that of a husband and wife settling in for the night and one leans into the other and says, "We need to find a way to save the house." They are not saying to each other, "Gosh. If only we could find the *10-Step Formula for Preserving Your Property*." They want to "save the house."

Over and over again, we've had prospects and clients convey two major concerns to us regarding asking for referrals: "I don't want to be pushy and hurt relationships" and "I don't want it to look like I'm begging." So now we take these concerns and use them in how we describe our training programs (live, video, and Internet based). We typically say, "You'll learn how to approach clients for referrals without pushing or begging."

Sometimes we take it a step further. We had a client who's been very successful with our video-based training program write to us, "Bill Cates makes asking for referrals as natural as breathing." Wow! It would be bragging if *I* said something like that about myself. When a *client* says it, it's very powerful. So we use the words our prospects and clients are using, and then we provide the solution to their concerns with other words our clients are using. This is a very powerful concept. Talk to your prospects and clients using the words that are already in their heads. They'll get what you do and how you can help them immediately.

ACTION STEP

As you meet with your clients, whether at regular business meetings or at a social lunch, talk to them about how they perceive your business. Talk to them about why they do business with you. What are the biggest problems you solve? If they were to talk to someone about you, what words would they use? Take what you learn and incorporate that into how you talk about your business to prospects over the phone and in person, as well as in your promotional literature and on your website.

ADDRESS CORE BENEFITS

Every business has some universal or core benefits it addresses with its clients. For example, in my business, helping people get more referrals is not the core benefit I help them achieve. Referrals are not the end product. Referrals are a means to the end—new clients. So when I am on the phone with prospective clients, while we certainly talk about my referral system and how they might implement it, it's all under the umbrella of client acquisition.

A financial advisor's core benefit isn't advice, as important as that is. It's what that advice does for the advisor's clients. It's the ability to help the clients to feel more secure or to fund their dreams. I have a friend who sells very sophisticated security software to large corporations and governments. His core benefit is a computer system that no one can break through. It's also peace of mind for the client. Don't ever discount the importance of peace of mind as one of your core benefits.

You might think that someone who sells printing is selling "quality ink on paper." And although print quality is very important, with today's technology it's almost a given. I think someone who is selling printing should address the core benefit of "what happens when things go wrong," meaning the willingness and ability to solve the problems that are inevitable in a customized manufacturing process like printing.

What are the core benefits you bring to your prospects and clients? Sometimes a core benefit involves solving a problem. Sometimes it involves taking advantage of an opportunity. Make sure you are crystal clear on how you serve your clients, and make that part of your opening conversation with new prospects. It will demonstrate that you know their business—which builds credibility and keeps the conversation alive.

PRESENT YOURSELF AS A SPECIALIST

Who gets paid more in our society—generalists or specialists? In his book *Telephone Sales for Dummies*, Dirk Zeller makes this powerful observation, "One of the best words you can use in describing your company or yourself is 'specialist.' It positions you as an expert. People want to work with the best and 'specialist' implies that you're more experienced in this particular field than others. Ultimately, it shows that the prospect has a low risk when choosing to work with you."

Who usually gets paid more, a specialist or a generalist? A specialist of course. A specialist not only conveys more perceived value but also brings more tangible value to the work he or she does. Another word you might use is *expert*. Position yourself as an expert in your field or even just a portion of your field.

I don't have to tell you how difficult it is to capture the attention of new prospects. This "specialist" or "expert" strategy is something I have used for over 18 years, and it has served me well to get my prospects to give me just enough time to start building value and piquing their interest.

QUESTIONS TO GET THE CONVERSATION STARTED

One key strategy in getting people to set an appointment with you is to create value and generate interest through the questions you ask. Asking prospects a question they don't know the answer to can be powerful, because it gets them thinking in ways they haven't thought before. Here are examples of questions that can be used to help you get the conversation started—along with some comments.

1. Getting more information from prospects may be as simple as repeating back their statement as a question. "You're trying to sell your business?" You can add the request, "Tell me more."

2. Question "fuzzy phrases" for clarification. Suppose they say, "I'm going to have to give this some thought." Then you say, "I understand. This is an important decision. As you give it consideration, can you tell me some of the things you'll be considering? What are some of the priorities you might be evaluating?" (Make this fit your business.)

3. Simple responses such as "Oh?" and "How so?" and "Tell me more" are just enough to keep them talking (and you learning).

4. Resist going into presentation mode after uncovering just a bit of a problem you think you can fix or need you can fill. Continue questioning to further develop the need or problem.

5. If you get a question you'd prefer to answer a bit later in the conversation, turn it around, but soften your delayed response by explaining why. "In order for me to suggest some specific things for you to do or how we might help you, I need to learn a few more key things. For instance . . ."

6. Start off with a common problem you solve. "Many of our clients come to us because they can't seem to _____. Is this a challenge for you?"

7. When talking to a prospect who either called you or agreed to take your call as the result of a referral, ask, "What did George say about me that caught your attention?"

8. Learn about other people directly or indirectly involved in the decision. When your prospect mentions other people, learn more. "Tell me more about Donna. How might she be involved in this decision?"

9. Be assumptive for a minute. "Let's say you've decided to bring in our video-training program. Who do you think would do the facilitation? Would that be you or someone else in your organization?"

10. If prospects have used a product or service similar to yours in the past, talk about how they made that decision and if they'd follow the same process this time around.

ACTION STEP

Make a list of all the questions you might want to ask your new prospects. You can even split the questions into categories. Have them printed out in checklist form and keep the list in front of you. Review the questions before you make the call so you know where you want to begin. Check off the questions as you ask them— taking notes on their answers, of course.

WHAT IS YOUR BODY OF EVIDENCE?

A big part of grabbing the attention of prospects and turning those prospects into clients is the body of evidence you bring to the table. This is especially important when selling a service, which is usually less tangible than a product. You are in the "evidence business." Here are the ingredients of a compelling body of evidence:

1. **Referrals.** A referral is great evidence! You know this. That's why you're reading this book.

2. **Testimonials.** Testimonials are a cousin of referrals. Third-party endorsements work. Do you have a system in place that generates testimonials on a regular basis?

3. **Special reports.** Use a special report to pique interest and bring value quickly.

4. **A great website.** Your branding (expertise) must be clear within the first few seconds. Video from you and testimonials from clients are key components.

5. **Case studies.** Communicating case studies to your prospects can be very compelling. You can put these case studies in your literature and on your website. And if you put them on your website, I urge you to consider using audio or video to relay this type of information. Your prospects can get a much better feel for you when they can hear your voice and even watch you. An easy way to do this is to record someone interviewing you about your product or service. You can cover the overarching philosophy of your business, describe the benefits of doing business with you, and then get into specific case studies where you have detected and solved client problems.

TESTIMONIALS—PART OF YOUR EVIDENCE

As I just mentioned, part of the body of evidence you want to have ready is testimonials. Testimonials—sometimes referred to as "third-party endorsements"—can often be the tool that tips the scales in your favor. I have become a testimonial-collecting machine over the years. Whenever people tell me they are producing tangible results with my system (which happens all the time), I ask them for a testimonial and their photo.

> *George, I'm glad you've been able to produce great results with our system. With your permission, I'd like to take your words from the e-mail you sent and craft a short statement from you that I might put on my website or use in some of my promotional literature. Would you be okay with that?*

I almost never hear no from the people I ask, and since I'm using their exact words (or very close to them), they almost never suggest any changes. After they've approved the statement, I solicit a photo.

> *George, thank you so much. One thing we like to do is place a small photo next to the statements, to make them as "real" as possible. Do you have a headshot of some sort you can send for this purpose?*

I get 99 percent of the photos I request. Some people have their colleague take a photo with their smartphone right on the spot. Since most of these statements are going on our website or other digital media, the quality doesn't need to be print quality, though I do get enough high-quality shots for brochures as well.

Survey Your Clients

Here's something I did recently that has turned out better than I ever expected. I sent an e-mail to the subscribers of my free e-mail newsletter (http://www.ReferralMinute.com). In exchange for responding to a short survey, I offered the recipients a free report and a chance at winning one of our larger training programs, the winner to be selected at random.

I asked them:

1. How were you doing with referrals before you learned my system?

2. What are you doing differently as the result of learning my system?

3. What results are you producing (please be as specific as possible)?

4. Can you quantify your results for me?

The net result was over 50 real-life success stories that specifically answered the questions I posed. These testimonials are making their way on to our website—some of them are associated with our specific referral tools and some just speaking to our system in general.

Can you do this with your clients? Of course you can! If you have a lot of clients, use e-mail and offer an incentive. If you have a small number of clients, just call them up and talk through it.

Collect Photos

If you visit our website (http://www.ReferralCoach.com), you'll see almost no testimonials without a photo next to them. Why? The more real your testimonial appears to the reader, the more effective it is. Which testimonial would you believe—one from *Peter F., Virginia*, or one from *Mollie Baker, Financial Advisor, McLean, VA*, with her photo next to it?

OFFER A FREE REPORT
TO PROSPECTS

One way to ease into a relationship with a new prospect and bring value quickly is to offer a free report, white paper, or e-book. Your first encounter with prospects, be it via e-mail or the phone, can be an offer to send them something of value. This is not your sales brochure. This free report should be 99 percent educational; it should be related to your product or service but still educational in nature. If you sell roofs, teach prospects how to buy a new roof—what to look for in a roofer and in a good roof. If you sell consulting, teach them how to select the best consultant. You get the idea.

A good title for such a report is often "How to Avoid the 10 Most Common Mistakes in Selecting a _____." You educate prospects on the potential problems and help them avoid those problems. It's a great one-two punch.

While this should be written in such a way that puts you and what you offer in a positive light, it should not be one long sales pitch.

If You Contact People in Their Homes

One side benefit of offering this free report, especially through an e-mail, is that if you sell to people in their homes (business to consumer), once they agree to receive the report, even if they are on the do-not-call list, you are now able to call them at home. As of the writing of this book, once people have raised their hands and said, "I'm interested," you may contact them on their home or cell phone for up to 18 months. (Personally I never call prospects on their cell phone unless I already have an established relationship and they have provided their cell phone number to me.)

ACTION STEP

What could your report be about? You're not a good writer? Go on the website http://www.elance.com and find someone to help you. You'd be surprised how affordable these folks can be. Come up with the gist of the report and have the person interview you. Your answers to their questions become the report. Keep it concise and conversational.

YOUR WEB PRESENCE WILL
HELP YOU GET THE APPOINTMENT

Having a good web presence is a big help in securing an appointment with your new prospects. When the prospects learn of you—even before you reach out to them—they may go to your website and also do an Internet search on your name and company. This is something I do with just about anyone I learn of—prospect, vendor, you name it. The better the web presence you project, the higher the credibility. The higher the credibility (from what the referral source says about you and how you show up from a web search), the more likely the prospect will take your call.

> **Website.** Your website needs to be up-to-date, professional, and easily accessible to the eye. By "accessible to the eye," I mean not cluttered or crammed. Many people try to accomplish too much on their home page and end up just confusing the visitors. You should have a very clear and concise branding promise and a testimonial or two (or "Praise for Our Work" button that takes them to many testimonials). You may also want to have a link to a free report or white paper that builds credibility through education.

> **Articles.** It's great to have articles you've written on your own website. What helps the web search even more is articles you've written that have been posted on other websites. When your prospect sees that others have featured your writing, that's a big plus for your credibility. Experts write. If you want to be perceived as an expert, you need to find ways to write about your area of expertise. Write and make yourself available as an expert in your field. If you write a blog, then your blog will likely show up on a web search.

> **YouTube.** Since Google owns YouTube and since Google is the number one search engine in the world (at this writing), your YouTube channel will likely show up high on a web search for you

and your company. Now your prospects get a chance to see and hear you either before you call them, which helps in securing the appointment, or after your first meeting, which helps you secure the business. Just make sure your videos are professional enough for your market.

LAY OUT THE OPTIONS

Here's a simple strategy I have found very effective with my first calls with new referral prospects. If you, like me, have different ways you serve your clients, you might find this idea helpful. For instance, with our corporate clients, we offer live speeches and training, video-based training (DVD or online), and virtual training (webinars and coaching calls). For individual salespeople, small business owners, and other professionals who sell, we offer boot camps, online video training, and a coaching program.

After I've asked the prospects some preliminary questions about their situation and the challenges they have that are related to my area of expertise, I tell them a little about each of the overall methods we have of helping them. I then ask them which method seems to resonate with them at the moment. Knowing what resonates with them early in the sales process allows me to focus on that area first. Once we've built the value of that method and the transformation (results) we believe we can help them produce, I may very well go back to the other two methods as a way of building the most effective transformational program. Of course, their budget may temper how big a program we build.

George, let me give you a quick overview of how we help companies like yours build highly productive and lasting referral cultures. You can then tell me which method seems to resonate with you the most. While we won't forget about the others, because sometimes a combination produces the best results, this will give us a place to start. How does that sound?

CONTACTING REFERRAL PROSPECTS

10

CONTACTING YOUR REFERRAL PROSPECT

Working from referrals and introductions gives you the advantage of already knowing something about your new prospect, so you can craft a more effective, tailored approach and, therefore, stand a better chance of actually reaching your prospects, getting them to take your call or reply to your voice mail or e-mail.

This chapter gives you many best practices that work well when working from referrals. You'll see how we use what we've learned from our referral source to maximize our appointment-setting efforts

HAVE A CLEAR GOAL FOR EVERY PHONE CALL

If you wing it when you call your new referral prospects—if you make it up as you go—you're going to be much less successful than if you have a clear goal for your call and a clear process designed to reach that goal.

Says Dirk Zeller, author of *Telephone Sales for Dummies*, "No matter how inconsequential you think a call may be, setting a goal for every call is important. Make your primary objective a tangible one; instead of 'Convince the prospect to consider my product further,' be sure an action is attached to it: 'Take an order.' 'Book an appointment.' 'Gather full profile from lead.' 'Ask all qualifying questions.' When you hang up the phone, you then have a material reflection of the results."

After I figure out my primary goal for my approach call, I come up with one or two secondary goals. For instance, if my goal is a face-to-face meeting and the prospect isn't ready for that, I may arrange a next phone call to keep the conversation going.

Every business is different, and so I can't tell you exactly what your goal should be, but here are a few classic examples:

1. **Get permission to send information.** Often referred to as call-mail-call, first you alert your prospects to the fact that you're sending them some information. That's an easy yes for them. Next you send the information. And then you follow up with a combination of e-mails and phone calls. If you find yourself having a decent initial conversation, meaning the prospect seems genuinely interested, you can often schedule the follow-up phone call at that moment. Sometimes, if the client's interest is strong enough, you can go for the appointment right then. Mail the information before the appointment or bring it with you.

2. **Learn a little and then schedule your next call.** At Referral Coach International, we are scheduling a lot of 5- to 10-minute initial calls. This is an easy yes for the new prospects. And it allows us to get the conversation started and begin to pique their interest. Though we are ready for a very short call, in most cases the prospects are open to the conversation and keep the conversation going themselves. *Gain an appointment.* Your goal may be to gain an appointment, and your secondary goal may be to send information and schedule the follow-up on the spot.

CALLING YOUR REFERRAL PROSPECTS—"LIKE OR ADMIRE"

In Section II, I covered certain types of information you can learn about your new referral prospect that only your referral source can give to you. Then, whenever possible, you can use that information in your initial phone call with your prospect to help you secure the appointment. I will illustrate each concept in a sample script. Of course, you will have to tailor this idea to fit the situation and your personality.

"Tell me something you like or admire about her?"

Good morning, Sandy. This is Bill Cates with RCI Financial. George Smith urged me to give you a call. I believe George has mentioned me to you?

(He sure has. He speaks very highly of you.)

And he speaks very highly of you. In fact, he told me you have one of the best business minds he's ever known. (With a smile in your voice) *Is George a reliable source in this matter?*

(Well you can't believe everything George says, but in this case I guess you can.)

I appreciate you taking my call. I know you're busy so I'll get right to the point . . .

If your referral source and prospect have a strong relationship where they kid each other—where you know you'll have a good reception on the other end—then don't hesitate to interject some humor. Keep it brief, but have some fun. As always, the situation and personalities should always rule.

CALLING YOUR REFERRAL PROSPECTS—
"WHAT'S IMPORTANT TO THEM"

Here's another strategy brought to life with a sample script. Your scripts will always vary depending on the situation and your personality.

"What's going on in his life that's important to him?"

Bob, George told me that you are a few months out from selling your business. Congratulations! Tell me, if you don't mind, a little bit about that.

(That's true. I've worked very hard the last 20 years to get to this point. It's pretty exciting for me—and a bit of a headache at the same time.)

I can imagine both of those feelings. One very strong area of my firm's expertise is in helping small business owners prepare for the sale of their business. There are some pretty important decisions you will need to be making over the coming months and beyond. I would like to present myself to you as a resource in this area. Would you be opening to continuing our conversation to see what that might look like?

Assuming the prospect is open to continuing the conversation, I would learn more about his situation before going for the appointment. You need to build some rapport and credibility with a high-level prospect such as this before suggesting the appointment.

CALLING YOUR REFERRAL PROSPECTS—
PRESENT YOURSELF AS A RESOURCE

When I'm contacting prospects for the first time, I almost always say something to the effect of "I'd like to present myself as a resource for you." I've found that the word resource works quite well in allowing me to be proactive but not pushy.

Hello Mrs. Smith. This is Bill Cates with RCI Financial. I know you're busy, but the reason I'm calling is because George Jones asked me if I'd give you a call. I believe he told you a little bit about me?

(Yes he did. I've been expecting your call.)

Good. I'm calling to present myself as an additional resource for you. George didn't tell me anything about your financial situation, so I'm not going to assume anything. I would, however, like to have a brief conversation just to see if I can be of service to you in some way and to determine if it makes sense for us to meet at some point.

Instead of just using the word *resource*, you may find it helpful to use the term *additional resource*. This approach is very nonthreatening and still proactive.

TO SCRIPT OR NOT TO SCRIPT, THAT IS THE QUESTION

Dirk Zeller, in his book *Telephone Sales for Dummies*, writes, "In order to meet your overall objectives, you want to take a few minutes before making a call to know what you're going to say and practice a little. What you say to the prospect is guided by your objective: If you're trying to determine whether the company is a good fit for your product, you prepare your list of qualifying questions. If you don't take a few moments to rehearse, you won't be prepared, and you risk blowing the call and blowing the lead, sometimes for good."

I'm a big advocate of not winging it when it comes to calling prospects on the phone—especially the very first call (or voice mail). I think you should know exactly what you plan to say, what questions you want to ask, and what objective you'd like to achieve from the call. The question at hand is, do you want to work from a sales script?

Here's what I do. Whenever I'm developing a part of my sales conversation, I always write it out at least once. I imagine I'm talking to a real prospect and write it up in a very conversational manner. Then I read it out loud a couple of times and tighten it up as I go. I then read it out loud a few more times until I "get it."

From there, I create a template of bullet points that match the sample conversation. This becomes my natural and genuine "script" for the call. I am now much less likely to forget all the things I wanted to say.

By truly knowing my exact track, I can actually be much more flexible in reacting to what my prospect throws at me. If you're stuck with a rigid script and don't really own your process and your objective, the unpredictable things that inevitably come up on your call can throw you off track big time. You may never recoup. Knowing your track will increase your flexibility, and you also become a better listener because you're not just focused on what you're going to say next.

ACTION STEP

To help you become natural and genuine with your script, use your own voice-mail system. It's an instant recording device at your disposal. Call your own number and leave yourself a voice mail covering what you plan on saying to your prospects. Then listen to it. Have others listen to it. Do you sound natural and genuine, or do you need to practice some more?

GETTING DOWN TO BUSINESS WITH REFERRAL PROSPECTS

During a referral seminar a participant came up to me at the break with a question. He told me that our referral system had changed his business forever, but he was stuck in one little place. Once on the phone with a new referral prospect, he sometimes had difficulty transitioning from the initial (rapport-building) part of the call into the business part of the call to present himself as a resource and, possibly, suggest an appointment.

Here is the approximate verbiage I gave to this gentleman. Perhaps you'll find a way to adopt this idea and adapt it to your business.

Good morning, Bob. This is Bill Cates with XYZ Financial. George Smith suggested I give you a call. I have to tell you, you have a real admirer in George. In fact, he told me you have one of the best business minds he's come across. Is George a trustworthy source on this matter?

(In this case, yes! You can believe George. He told me to expect your call.)

That's good. Look, Bob, I don't know if I can be an additional resource for you or not, but based on George's satisfaction with my work and his recommendation that we talk, here's what I'm hoping for from this brief first conversation. I'd like to ask you a few questions and tell you a little bit about the value I believe I provide. After 10 minutes or so, we'll both be able to decide if it makes sense to continue the conversation—either through another phone call or getting together. How's that sound?

This is a simple way to transition from the initial rapport-building part of the phone call into the business portion of the call. I'm not expecting you to use these exact words (though you can if you wish). It's the transition that many people have difficulty with. I hope this helps a bit.

ACTION STEP

Get clear on your transitions. This is important for your phone calls as well as every other aspect of your sales process. You want to be able to move fluidly from one part of your conversation to the next. If not, your awkwardness may show through as a lack of confidence.

CAN YOU USE HUMOR WITH PROSPECTS?

The answer to the above question is absolutely yes! I have an opportunity to speak to many very high-level prospects, and I've found that having a little fun on the phone is always appreciated. You have to be authentic and appropriate with your prospects (and their relationship with the referral source).

But First . . .

You better ask your referral source a few questions first:

- "How do you know her? Can you tell me the nature of your relationship with her?"

- "Can you give me a sense of her personality?"

- "Tell me something you like or admire about her."

- "You know I like to have a little fun in my conversations. Do you think she would be receptive to that right away, or should I be all business?"

Armed with this information, I know how much humor I can interject.

For Example

Upon asking a client (who is giving me a referral), "What do you like or admire about Brian Bishop?" my client said, "He's got a great sense of humor. He's got a million jokes and fun stories. Tell him to tell you the 'preacher story.'"

Then, upon calling the prospect, I said, "George told me I should ask you to tell me the preacher story." My new prospect howled with laughter. He asked me if I had the time. Of course I did. He told me a very funny story. We both had a good laugh, and getting down to business was the next logical step.

Another Place for Humor

Once I've had at least one conversation with an interested prospect, but I can't seem to get the prospect to return my call, I've had great success sending a funny e-mail to the person. I use a multiple-choice format such as:

> Chris, I'm having a little difficulty reaching you and wanted to know how you'd like to proceed. Please reply to this e-mail and check the box that applies to you. Thanks!
>
> ___ I'm still interested. Please reach out to me around _____.
>
> ___ I've been in the Amazon jungle for two weeks. Give me another week to recover from the snakebite and reach out to me again.
>
> ___ My mother-in-law is in town threatening to move in with us. Can you help me with this challenge first?
>
> ___ Give me a couple of days. I'll get back to you. Promise!
>
> ___ I'm not really a good prospect for you at this time.

As with all the strategies in this book, the relationship is king, meaning the type of rapport and trust you've built up—along with knowing the personality of the prospect—will allow you to determine how far to go in using humor.

Disclaimer: And if you don't have a good sense of humor? Well, these strategies are not for you. Play it straight.

MAKE TIME FOR SETTING APPOINTMENTS

I can't tell you how many people I meet who seem to have all sorts of excuses about why they're not calling their referral prospects. None of the excuses make sense. And remember, if you're not calling your referral prospects, you're burning your referral bridge between you and your referral source.

If you have trouble finding the time to make your prospecting calls, make an appointment with yourself and respect that appointment as if it's an appointment with a client. Dirk Zeller says, "Prospects represent future revenue for your business, so they are every bit as important as current clients."

I suggest you batch your phone calls; schedule phone-calling time for yourself. If you're not doing this, find someone to hold you accountable to this business-building behavior.

I used to procrastinate with my writing (books, articles, news-letters). I told this to the members of my business study group, so they suggested I set a goal with some accountability. I agreed to write eight full days in the coming three months. For each day I missed, I would put $250 into the group's kitty. At our next meeting I wrote a check for $750. I missed three days. My colleague (and friend) Steven Gaffney immediately said, "Obviously the penalty wasn't enough." And, of course, he was right. The point isn't to write the check; it's to make the goal. I upped the amount to $500 per day and haven't missed a day since—$500 got my attention.

What will it take for you to make sure you schedule enough time for setting appointments (or addressing any other part of the sales process you're letting fall through the cracks)?

DEALING WITH THE BRUSH-OFF FROM NEW REFERRAL PROSPECTS

Even referral prospects can give you the brush-off if you don't approach them properly:

- "I'm not interested."

- "I'm happy with the person I'm using."

- "You've caught me at a bad time."

- "We don't need [or use] _____."

I remember calling a prospect in Phoenix. His brush-off was "Referrals don't work in Phoenix." Man, was I caught off guard with that one. I'd never heard that before. Everyone I called always knew the value of referrals. I was just getting started in my new business, so I admit I didn't handle it very well. I don't know if he really believed that or was just testing me. I did say, "Really? I've not heard that before. Tell me more"—which is a pretty good initial response to most objections. The truth is, he wasn't interested and made it pretty clear quickly.

When you work from referrals, and especially introductions, your percentage of brush-offs or knee-jerk reactions will diminish significantly. Much of what's covered in this book can directly or indirectly help you reduce the chances for a negative knee-jerk reaction on the part of your prospect:

1. Work from high-level referrals. The higher the trust between the referral source and the prospect, the better initial reaction you will get.

2. Turn referrals into introductions. When the prospect knows who you are, why you're calling, and a little about the good work you do, brush-offs are rare.

3. Ask your referral source, "How do you think he'll react to this introduction?" This might give you a sense of the personality you will encounter.

4. Ask your source, "Do you know whom she might be using currently?" This can help you prepare your approach to this prospect.

5. Present yourself as a "resource" or as an "additional resource." Don't come on too strong, but be confident in your ability to add something to the prospect's situation.

6. Do your homework. The more you learn about the prospect— from your referral source and the Internet—the better opening

statement you will have. Learning what the referral source likes or admires about the prospect almost always eliminates the negative knee-jerk reaction.

7. Prepare for the phone call. Think through your opening statement and initial questions. Don't wing it!

8. Send (via e-mail) a little something of value before you call; for example, send a special educational report or a link to a short educational video (not promotional material— educational material).

So what would have helped me with this prospect in Phoenix? Well, just about everything in the above list. When you do get the brush-off, try not to let it get to you. Acknowledge it and then ask a question. Sometimes just saying, "Oh?" or "Tell me more" will get you past the knee-jerk response. Sometimes it won't. Sorry, nothing works all the time. Don't you just hate that?

LEAVE A VOICE-MAIL MESSAGE THAT GETS RETURNED

Jill Konrath, in her book *Selling to Big Companies* (Dearborn; http://www.SellingtoBigCompanies.com), provides these tips for getting your prospects to return your voice-mail messages. I personally use several of these ideas and find them very effective, and they work with referral prospects as well as other types of prospects.

1. **Get down to business right away.** Your prospects don't like phony friendliness. Instead, be professional and state, "Eric, Jill Konrath calling. 123-456-7890. The reason for my call is [state a compelling benefit or idea]."

2. **Reference any referrals up front.** The single best way to keep prospects listening is to mention the name of a

respected colleague. Make sure you state this person's name immediately: "Pat Jones suggested I call you."

3. **Show you've done your homework.** Let prospects know you prepared for their call by researching their business. Tell them if you've worked with other similar people or companies. You might say, "I was on your website and noticed . . ." or "In working with other CPA firms, I know they're struggling with . . ."

4. **Mention a recent newsworthy event.** Bring up recent events that create a need relevant to your offering. This includes things like third-quarter earnings, new management, acquisitions, downsizings, higher interest rates, or new strategic initiatives. Let the prospects know this is what triggered the call.

5. **State a strong value proposition.** Prospects are always interested in the business outcomes you can deliver. Instead of talking about your product or service, use business terminology and metrics: "We help companies shrink time to revenue on new product launches by up to 47 percent."

6. **Share a fresh perspective.** Nothing is more tempting than ideas, insights, or information that can help prospects eliminate their problems or achieve their objectives: "I have some ideas on speeding up your sales cycle" or "We recently did a study of CFOs' primary concerns in today's business environment."

7. **Eliminate any self-serving verbiage.** Much as you might like to talk about your state-of-the-art systems, unique methodologies, and passion for excellence, it turns your prospects off. Get rid of all self-promotion puffery, creative crap, and technical tripe.

8. **Sound like a trusted peer.** Today's buyers want to work with savvy sellers who bring personal value to the relationship.

Don't sound like you're hoping to meet with them or grateful for even 10 minutes of their time. Instead, talk like you would if you called a colleague with an idea.

9. **Use a script as a foundation.** Without an outline, you'll ramble on and on, which virtually guarantees you'll be deleted. You have 30 seconds max on a voice mail. Every word counts, so make sure you get it right. If you get deleted, you've blown the opportunity.

CAN YOU HAVE FUN IN A VOICE MAIL?

I know that Jill Konrath advises, "Get down to business right away." And that's what I usually do. However, when working from referrals, you can often have some fun with your new prospects, if you know their personality and the nature of their relationship with the referral source.

Here's a real-life example. I got a referral from Ray Johnson to Milton Brooks. I asked Ray, "Tell me something you like or admire about Milton." Ray said, "Milton has more integrity than anybody I've ever met. He's a stand-up guy!" Nice!

I called Milton and got his voice mail. My message went something like this: "Milton, this is Bill Cates with Referral Coach International. Ray Johnson told me to give you a call. I have to say, you have a real admirer in Ray. He said some pretty nice things. Tell you what . . . I'll fill you in on what he said when we speak." Do you think I created some fun curiosity with this message?

Milton called me back and got my voice mail. "Bill, this is Milton Brooks. You can't believe a thing Ray Johnson says. I'm in all week. Give me a call." Now I know we're having fun.

I finally reached Milton. "Milton, I can't believe a thing Ray says?" (No response.) "Ray said you had more integrity than anyone else he's ever met. He said you're a stand-up guy!"

Long pause. "Well, I guess you can believe a few things he says."

ACTION STEP

Have fun with referrals! If you're not having fun, you're probably just not doing it enough.

E-MAIL PROSPECTING TIPS

Jill Konrath, author of *SNAP Selling* (Penguin; http://www.SNAP Selling.com), shares these tips for sending e-mails to prospects:

- **Length.** Keep your prospecting e-mails under 90 words. Shorter is nearly always better when dealing with today's crazy-busy prospects. Remember that many people are reading your messages in their preview screen or on their mobile device. They hate scrolling, and worse, they hate rambling messages.

- **Look.** Simple text (black and white) messages are essential when reaching out to a new person. If you have fancy templates, save them for your friends or family. They don't evoke the image of a highly capable resource. Also, think carefully before using logos, and definitely avoid using colored fonts. Logos and colors, especially red, catch the eye of spam blockers.

- **Links.** If you have some good resources on your website that you want to drive your prospects to, only send one link per e-mail. People will look at one link, but more than that sends them into overwhelm. Future e-mails can include the additional links.

- **Referrals.** If you've got a referral or useful name, by all means use it in your subject line. It's the ultimate way to get a quick reply. Subject lines that address immediate concerns, company changes, or critical business issues are also highly effective.

GET PROSPECTS TO RETURN
YOUR CALL OR E-MAIL

You've got the referral. You've even turned it into an introduction. Now you have to get your new prospect to return your voice mail or e-mail.

Go for a Five-Minute Phone Call

I believe that most people try to go too far too fast with their new prospects—especially the really busy prospects (which seems to be just about everyone these days). Try making your first contact a five-minute phone call. That's it! In your e-mail or voice-mail message, tell the prospect that all you need is five minutes of his or her time: "I'd like to present myself as a resource for your company. Can we set up a five-minute phone call to get the conversation started? That's it. Five minutes. From there we can decide what our next step should be." This becomes an easier yes for your prospect.

Make It a Productive Call

Planning your call will lead to a more productive call.

> **Minute 1.** Acknowledge the referral source, the referral source and prospect's relationship, and perhaps the reason the referral source thought this would be a valuable call for the prospect.

> **Minutes 2 to 4.** Ask the prospect a question or two. Ideally, your referral source told you one or two things of importance in the prospect's life or business, and your products and services can have a positive impact in those areas. Craft a question or two that helps you make that connection. Or have a couple of generic questions that have proved to stimulate further conversation.

George said that you're looking to retire in about three years. Is that an accurate time frame, and have you sat down to figure out how you will maximize your income once you retire?

(If yes.) *How confident do you feel in your ability to execute your plan?* (Again, you'll have to come up with questions that fit your business.)

Minute 5. Suggest a next step. When you dial the phone number, have a next-step goal in mind. It could be to get the prospect to accept information you'd like to mail that fits his or her situation. It could be to set up an in-person meeting. It could be to schedule another, longer, phone call. Have a goal in mind and be ready to be flexible.

Bob, based on this quick conversation, as well as George's recommendation, I suggest we schedule a time where we can examine your situation in more detail. It's very possible I can become a valuable resource for you in this area. Shall we look at our calendars?

Perhaps you're feeling too limited by this 5-minute call. Try asking for 5 to 10 minutes. Try asking for 7 minutes (that will look a little different). The point is to create a situation to get an easy yes to your request for a little bit of the prospect's time.

Of course, the more credible the referral source and the better the introduction, the easier all this will go.

ACTION STEP

Create an agenda for a five- to seven-minute phone call. Role-play it once or twice with someone. Now you'll feel confident asking for a very short phone appointment.

COULD YOUR FIRST
APPOINTMENT BE ONLINE?

Even if you live in the same city as your prospect, consider holding your first meeting online via Skype or one of the many online meeting or webinar services available. This option will allow you to connect with your prospect in a more substantial way than just a telephone appointment, and it will save on driving time. Of course, if you are doing business nationally or internationally, you are probably already using this option. Using Skype or another online service provides the opportunity for videoconferencing and showing visuals (like Power-Point slides). Connecting with video usually helps with the rapport- and trust-building process.

Here are a few tips for having a smooth and productive online appointment:

1. Work from an agenda, just as you would with any other meeting. Let your prospects know you have an agenda. If appropriate, share the agenda with the participants ahead of time so that they can provide feedback and make adjustments. You can even provide your prospects with some of the questions you intend to ask them, so they can be well prepared.

2. If there are any printed materials involved, confirm all parties are in possession of these materials the day before. If the materials are essential to a good call, reschedule the call until they arrive.

3. Limit your online appointments to 60 minutes or less. Try not to cover too much in your first appointment, unless your prospect is extremely interested in what you offer and is already in "buying mode." I've run online appointments as short as 10 minutes that have been very effective in generating the next step.

4. As with all appointments (live, phone, or online), do your best to have all the decision makers present. One good thing about online appointments is that you can record them, and so a decision maker (or member of your team) could view the appointment later if he or she were so inclined.

Whatever technology you choose to use, don't use it for the very first time with a prospect. Practice using the technology a few times before trying it with a prospect or client. You want the technology to serve your purpose, not become a distraction.

GET PROSPECTS ENGAGED IN YOUR MATERIALS OR WEBSITE

Given the nature of the work I do, I have very few in-person appointments. Almost all my appointments are over the phone or use some sort of web-based meeting software. I've found that getting my prospects engaged in the materials I've already sent to them or having them look at certain pages on my website seems to get them more involved. I believe the visual aspect of the sales process is very important.

If you have enough time on your first call, find ways to engage your prospects in your materials. If you sent them printed literature, call their attention to one or more portions of that material. You will find it helpful to put sticky arrows or other such identifiers on the material so that when you direct the prospects over the phone, they will have no difficulty finding the right spot. (Don't use the sticky arrows that say "sign here." You'll scare people off.)

If the prospects have access to the Internet (which most people will have unless you've reached them on their cell phone), then get them engaged in portions of your website. You can either direct them yourself or, better yet, use an online technology such as GoToMeeting, Webex, or one of the many other services so the prospects can view your computer screen as you walk them through parts of your website or other materials.

There are three benefits to engaging your prospects in this way:

1. People tend to learn faster and retain more through visual rather than auditory means.

2. They will get a clearer picture (literally) of what you are explaining to them. Your words will make more sense when they have a visual representation of those words.

3. The act of engaging them in this way gives you more opportunities for rapport and trust building, as well as opportunities for humor.

ACTION STEP

Don't let the first time you try this idea be with a real-life prospect. Practice every single part of your phone appointments and in-person appointments with a colleague, manager, or friend. Don't ever practice on prospects and clients!

REDUCE APPOINTMENT CANCELLATIONS

Some industries encounter the challenge of appointment cancellations and no-shows. Of course, the first line of defense in preventing this time-wasting, energy-zapping dynamic is to make sure your prospect has a strong sense of the value you provide, has an appreciation of the problems you solve, and is highly interested in meeting with you. This is always the first place to look when someone cancels an appointment and doesn't want to reschedule.

Another strategy that can often reduce no-shows and cancellations is sending something of value to the prospect before your appointment. Now I'm not talking about bribes or other items of a personal nature that can get the prospect and you in a questionable situation. Here are a few things I've seen others provide in their efforts to reduce cancellations and no-shows:

1. Educational report, printed or electronic (purely educational—not a sales tool).

2. A printed book related to your prospect's business or industry.

3. Something fun like a mug with candy in it or Girl Scout cookies your daughter is selling.

4. A list of resources that the prospect might find helpful, related or unrelated to your core product or service.

5. A fun, customized greeting card that you create online but that gets mailed to the prospect (with brownies or cookies, if you wish). I use SendOutCards for this all the time. To check out the service and send yourself a free sample card, go to http://www.SendOutCards.com/billcates.

STAYING IN TOUCH WITH PROSPECTS

11

KEEPING THE COURTSHIP ALIVE

With most businesses, *when* someone becomes interested in speaking, setting an appointment, or doing business with you is truly a matter of timing. For some of my largest clients, it's taken three to five years to get the ball rolling on substantial business. I have a colleague whose motto is "I'll prospect them until they buy or die!" Perhaps a little extreme, but we get the point. Most businesses need a model of staying in touch with prospects. When the prospect is a referral prospect and we have learned that he or she truly is a good match for us, it makes sense to keep the courtship alive—for at least a while.

And it is a courtship, kind of like dating. As in dating, you can't come on too strong, and yet you have to remain interested. You never know when the other party is going to take a step in your direction. As I was conducting my preprogram research with a new client, I discovered that the client's company had many sources of good leads. It was getting its fair share of referrals without asking for them, and it had some Internet marketing programs that were getting a large number of prospects to raise their hands and say, "I'm interested." Yet the company lacked any systems to stay in touch with these interested parties after one (yes, just one) attempt to reach them. I could only imagine how much business it was losing by this shortsighted approach. Of course, I helped the client put a simple but effective system in place. The company's sales increased by 43 percent!

Professional persistence is a critical key to success in client acquisition. This chapter will give you some great ideas to keep your courtships with prospects alive and to turn those prospects into new clients.

PLAN FOR MULTIPLE TOUCHES

Jill Konrath, author of *SNAP Selling*, writes, "From the onset, you need to plan a minimum of 8–12 touches. You can call people up. Send them letters. Invite them to events. Share good information with them. But think in terms of multiple contacts from the get-go. That way you're not disappointed when you don't get immediate results. And, you can spread your message (key points, value proposition, expertise) over time in the various mediums you use."

Here are nine ideas to pick from to keep your courtship of big prospects alive over time:

1. Send them something of value, perhaps an article you wrote (or a book or report). My company has a series of referral tip sheets we send to prospects over a year's time.

2. Invite them to an educational event (live or online webinar). Many companies like to host educational events for their clients and prospects. Sometimes this is an easier way for your prospects to get a sense of you and the work you do without having to sit down face-to-face, knowing you'll be asking them to do business with you.

3. Invite them to a social event. As with educational events, many companies host client appreciation events, to which they also invite prospects. Now the prospects get to

experience the type of relationships you have with your clients.

4. Sign them up for your newsletter (e-mail, blog, or paper). Putting prospects, with their permission, onto an e-mail newsletter is usually a pretty easy thing to do. Since "open rates" for e-mail newsletters continue to go down, many companies are returning to mailing printed newsletters so that they stand out and get read.

5. Make quick value-oriented phone calls. Keep looking for information related (and unrelated) to your core product or service that your prospects might find interesting or helpful. Call them now and then with this information. You never know when you might hear, "Funny you should call. Your timing is perfect. We were just discussing you."

6. Call with "curiosity questions" that might expose a weakness in their current system or strategies.

7. Offer a "free coaching" session. This is something we do at RCI. When people experience our value firsthand, they are often interested in knowing how else we can help them. They get a "free taste" of our value—like the bourbon chicken samples that are handed out on toothpicks at the mall food court.

8. Create a VIP list for your most important prospects. Send them something of educational value or fun on a regular basis. At RCI, we have several lists of VIPs to whom we mail educational or fun items. One of the most well-received items was a box of Girl Scout Thin Mints. (Needless to say, my daughter sold the most boxes of cookies in her troop that year.)

9. Invite them (and their family and friends) to participate in a community service event. Many prospects and clients like the opportunity to give back to the community and get their children involved.

ACTION STEP

Don't wing it when it comes to staying in touch with prospects. Lay out a plan and follow it. Keep making it better.

MAKE IT EASY TO REMAIN PERSISTENT

I don't know about you, but whenever I don't keep good records of my conversations with prospects, my efforts to remain in touch in an effective way seem to fizzle. Relying on my memory just doesn't cut it. How about you?

To "keep the sale alive," we must be in the habit of keeping good records of our conversations. We have to have enough detail so we remember the flow of our conversations. Once we get to the point of not remembering what we said or they said on the last call, we won't feel confident picking up the phone. It will be awkward. We won't know how to add value. The prospecting process dies.

Preplan Your Next Step

One solid habit I've been able to establish is the habit of planning my next contact either before I finish the call with the prospect (something we figure out together) or right after the call ends (part of keeping good records). Sometimes—especially when the prospects are genuinely interested, but it's a timing issue—you can work with them to determine the next time and reason for the next call.

Have a Solid Reminder System in Place

What system do you use to make sure no prospects fall through the cracks? I hope you're not relying on a paper system anymore. Okay . . .

paper systems have worked for hundreds of years, but I think you'd be silly not to take advantage of all the efficiencies computers offer in this area.

As mentioned above, after each call with a new prospect, I plan my next strategy. I figure out the timing for the next contact, and then I set a reminder that pops up at the appropriate time. In this way, I can let go of that prospect for the time being, knowing that no one will drop through the cracks.

I happen to use Microsoft Outlook for this. My director of sales and marketing uses ACT. At the time of writing this book, we are about to switch to a program called Infusionsoft. There are many great systems out there. Use one! Never, ever rely on your memory.

BE A NUDGE— BUT WITH A PURPOSE

When you follow up with prospects, do you have a better reason than "I'm just checking in." While I'm as guilty of this weak sort of follow-up call as the next person, I know that it's not the best way to go.

Nudge with Value

These days, when I follow up with prospects who should have gotten back to me—per our verbal agreement from our previous call—but didn't, I nudge them by providing some value at the same time. For instance, I have a number of referral tip sheets I've created as PDFs. When I reach out to prospects with an e-mail, I always attach another tip sheet for them. I'll say, "Attached is our Referral Tip Sheet #3 for you to share with all your reps. I'm looking forward to our next conversation. Can we get it scheduled this week?" And per the previous strategy, I keep track of what I send to them.

Yes, I'm nudging the process, but doing so with value and with purpose.

Nudge with Scarcity

Sometimes you can move a prospect into action by creating a situation of scarcity. For example, I limit myself to no more than five out-of-town presentations per month. So when I follow up with people who expressed interest in having me speak at their conference or come in for a full training session, I will let them know my number. "George, as you recall, I can commit to five speaking engagements per month. I just booked another event for October. While the last thing I want to do is pressure you and your committee, I do want to remain available for your conference. Have you made a decision yet? Do you have a sense of when you will? Shall we get on the phone soon to further discuss my program and the benefits to your reps?"

Debbi is a very high-level financial advisor who uses this approach. She has the capacity for about 20 new clients per year. She lets her clients and prospects know this on a fairly regular basis (without being obnoxious about it). This scarce-resource approach has her clients saying, "She only takes on a few new clients each year. She's very selective." And it gets her prospects saying, "Do you think she'd take a look at our situation?"

ACTION STEP

Create an inventory of a few things that you can use to nudge with value. They can be purely digital in format. And think of a way you can create scarcity in how you talk about your value. Be careful with scarcity, however. This scarcity needs to be real, not something you're making up just to move people to a decision.

USE EVENTS TO CONNECT WITH REFERRAL PROSPECTS

In Section II, I discussed how events can be used to create introductions from clients to prospects in a social or educational environment.

You can also use events as a strategy to remain in contact with prospects. These events can be educational (value added) or fun (building rapport and trust through social interaction).

For example, Russ is a financial advisor near Houston. Since he's quite adept at generating a steady flow of referral prospects, he always has an "inventory" of prospects he just can't seem to meet with or move forward in their relationship. So he hosts social events (like wine tastings) just for these prospects. No clients allowed—just referral prospects. At his last event, he had 19 referral prospects attend, and 7 of them moved forward to become clients. Once they met him in a low-key social setting, they felt more comfortable moving into a business conversation.

KEEP THE FLOW OF VALUE GOING—CREATE VIP LISTS

I believe that a critical element in keeping referral prospects in your pipeline is the concept of "creating a flow of value." We must continue to look for various ways to add value to the relationship. If you aren't looking to add value with each phone call—and even between phone calls—then why are you even contacting people? You can't keep calling them and asking, "Are you ready to meet with me now?" or some similar silly question.

Most effective prospectors work several contact strategies at the same time. For instance, you might put your prospects on a list to receive your monthly newsletter or weekly tips. Electronic methods have their place, but they aren't usually enough.

As previously mentioned, at Referral Coach International we've created several VIP lists totaling over 300 high-level prospects, clients, and COIs. We send them something of value on a regular basis. (Yes! We use regular mail or sometimes UPS.) Over the years we've mailed books, audio CDs, DVDs, reports, checklists, lists of resources, etc. We are always working about two to three months in advance so we don't have to rush anything. Some lists get something once per month and other lists once per quarter. We've even created a special sticker that goes on the outside of the envelope and package letting recipients know that they are one of our VIPs. In addition, we've had other companies that are trying to reach our market provide us with items of value to send to our VIPs.

GO FOR THE NO

While I believe in being professionally persistent with referral prospects, I don't like to beat a dead horse, so to speak. If my prospect shows interest and responds favorably to my continued contact, I remain in touch.

When I have a prospect that seems to have no interest, I usually do one of three things:

1. I stop contacting the prospect and free up my time and energy to focus on generating new prospects and serving my current clients.

2. When I have a prospect that I know I can help or who represents a large amount of business for my company, I look for other people to refer me to this prospect again. Many times I find someone else who knows this prospect, and I ask the person to put a good word in for me. This is often all it takes to get the prospect active again.

3. I go for the no. This is a technique I learned from the late, great sales trainer Dave Sandler. When I have a prospect who keeps putting me off, I say something like, "George, please tell me if I'm wrong, but I'm getting the impression that we may never have the opportunity to do business together. Do you think that's true?" Sometimes my prospect says yes, and I'm "free"! And sometimes my prospect lets me know he or she is still interested and often reveals new information that allows us to keep the courtship alive.

Only when you come from a place of abundance—trusting your ability to generate many new prospects—will you have no difficulty with this strategy. When you come from abundance, you're never afraid of "no."

ACTION STEP

Look at your pipeline of prospects. Can you get referred to them again from another source? Or who among them should you go for the no? It could be time to free up your time and mental energy for some fresh prospects.

SECTION IV
GET MORE CLIENTS
Confirm the New Relationship with
High-Value Clients

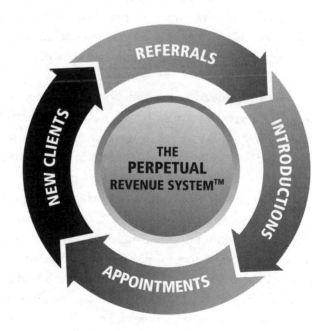

A NEW WAY TO
LOOK AT SELLING

What is your relationship to selling? Do you get energized by moving someone along in your process and bringing that person on as a new client? Or do you see *sales* as a dirty word and not consider yourself a salesperson? On either account, I think you're going to appreciate the following perspective.

Some people view selling in terms such as *manipulation* and *pushing*. Personally, I like to think of selling as *positive influence*. We form a relationship with new prospects and help them, advise them, influence them in their decision-making process. And we do it in a way where we're always looking out for what's best for the prospect.

I think that we accomplish this positive influence through building trust and then moving through a process that's made up of a series of *permissions* or *invitations*. We gain permission to ask some questions, the answers to which not only inform us, but also, we hope, teach our prospects. We invite our prospects to continue the conversation when we send them information, make another phone call, or have an in-person meeting.

We continue to gain permission from our prospects to probe, and in our efforts we learn to be a resource for them. We invite them to take a look at how we might serve them. The combination of building trust and providing value along the way is what allows this process to continue moving forward.

I also like the word *brainstorm* when talking about selling. What if in your conversations with a new prospect, you invite the prospect to brainstorm about his or her situation. "Neither of us is certain if I can be a valuable resource for you just yet. Based on what Bob said about your situation, I suspect I can. But first let's brainstorm a little to see what that might look like. As we exchange information and ideas, I think the answer will become clear."

We're being proactive but not pushy. We're inviting them into a no-pressure conversation to see what the possibilities may be.

I'm not saying you don't want to have a sales process or plan to help you move a person from prospect to client—if it's a good match.

Of course you do! Just do it in a way that's refreshing to your prospects. Invite them into a *conversation*.

Sales and personal growth expert Brian Tracy (http://www .BrianTracy.com) says, "Top sales professionals see themselves as 'Doctors of Selling.' They see themselves as professionals, well educated, acting in their 'patient's' best interest, and bound by a high code of ethics."

Like a doctor, a sales professional starts with the examination, which determines the diagnosis, which leads to the prescription. Each of these steps takes place through a series of permission asked for by the salesperson and granted by the prospect.

Closing Versus Confirming

Many people engaged in the sales process talk in terms of "closing the sale." I like to think in terms of "confirming the relationship." When the prospect decides to work with us, we're not closing the relationship. And in most cases, we're not closing the sales process either. We're confirming the new relationship and moving forward with the delivery of the product or service. You may find me using the word *closing* from time to time in this book, but please know that I'm always referring to confirming the new relationship.

In this fourth and final section of the book, I will provide you with many proven strategies and tactics designed to help you confirm more new relationships. And by working through referrals, this confirming process is almost always easier.

BUILDING TRUST

12

CREATING TRUST

If there is any one element that *must* be present in a successful sales situation, it's trust. And since referrals are *borrowed trust*, you enter all your new relationships at a higher point of trust.

- Trust allows the prospect to give you an appointment.

- Trust allows you to ask probing questions.

- Trust allows you to keep the sale moving forward.

- Trust allows the prospect to say yes to becoming a client.

- Trust is what allows your clients to accept your recommendations.

- Trust is what keeps your clients doing business with you.

- Trust is what generates referrals.

- Trust allows the cycle to repeat over and over again.

Michael Vickers, in his book *Becoming Preferred: How to Outsell Your Competition*, lays out what he calls a "new model of selling." In this model, Vickers says that "40% of the sales process is based in building trust with your prospect. Features, benefits, and confirming the business are still an important part, but pale in comparison to the importance of building trust."

Trust is not an easy thing to build quickly, but we need to focus on this and do our best. This chapter will stimulate your thinking and, I hope, your actions to build deeper trust with both prospects and clients. Do this and, according to Vickers, you're 40 percent there.

ASKING GOOD QUESTIONS BUILDS TRUST

Chapter 13 is devoted to asking questions, but let's relate that strategy in this chapter to building trust. Notice in the heading above that I said "good" questions. What do I mean by that? I mean questions that go beyond the surface level of basic information. For instance, let's say you're a financial advisor. As you are learning about you client's priorities, problems, and plans for the future, you might hear your client say something like, "We want to be able to do what we want, when we want, without being too worried about budgets." Okay, that's nice information to have, but you want to take a closer look at that statement by asking, "What are some of the things you foresee yourself doing?" and "Why is this important to you?" These types of questions do three things. First, they demonstrate that you care and that you want to know what's important to the client. Second, they will help you determine if you can help the client or if the client has unrealistic expectations. Third, just helping people get really clear on their financial future is a valuable process for most. Can you see how going deeper with your questions (and you can go even deeper than this) will help you build trust?

ACTION STEP

Think about the questions you typically ask and the answers you typically get. Are you going one, two, or three steps deeper? Are you demonstrating a sincere interest in a client's situation by wanting to learn more?

LISTENING WELL BUILDS TRUST

Okay, you already know that you need to be a good listener. Gretchen, a financial advisor in Fairfax, Virginia, knew this too, and yet she told me she didn't have a clue about how much she talked during her appointments until she had a bad case of laryngitis. For two days she ran appointments without being able to say much. She realized that these were some of the best appointments she ever had. She learned more about her clients, and her clients really felt listened to.

Joey, a consultant near Houston, tells me that he never takes notes while a client is speaking. He just listens. Once the client is finished, he picks up his pen and paper and writes what he thought he heard, running it by the client as he writes. In this way, Joey really lets the client know he's listening and truly wants to get it right.

Stop talking! I don't mean to be harsh, but most people just talk too much on their calls and appointments. People get into the presentation mode too quickly. We get the answer to a question and then "present" to that. Slow down! Ask questions. Per the previous strategy, ask follow-up questions to gain clarity and go deeper. And then listen. Stop listening to respond, and just listen to understand.

ALWAYS LEADING WITH VALUE BUILDS TRUST

If you ever stopped to think about the people in your life that you trust—particularly in business—I bet one of the common denominators for all those relationships would be that they happily *serve* you in some way. It seems to be human nature to begin to trust people who serve us, who give of themselves without always expecting compensation. So, to once again employ that useful term from *Star Trek*, your "prime directive" should be always to lead with value. Before any appointment with a prospect or client, stop and think, "How can I bring some extra, unexpected value to this person on this appointment?"

Of course, there are many ways to bring value, including asking probing questions that get your clients thinking in ways they haven't thought before. Another way is to help them with something that has little or nothing to do with your core product or service. Still another way to serve them is to give them referrals that help them—either prospects for their business or other service providers that can be a resource for them.

ACTION STEP

What are two probing questions you can ask prospects that they will not likely know the answer to but will get them thinking in new ways?

TELLING THE TRUTH BUILDS TRUST

While I suspect there are some salespeople and other professionals who out-and-out lie to their prospects and clients, this is not what I mean by "telling the truth." In this context, I mean not withholding information that you think the clients need to hear, even if they might not like it. The respect and esteem your clients hold for you will usually increase when they know that you are being completely forthcoming with them, that you're not holding anything back. I believe that, if expressed in the right way, we can say just about anything we need to say to another person. It's all in the words we choose and the manner of our delivery.

DISCUSSING EXPECTATIONS BUILDS TRUST

I hope that you are in the habit of talking to prospects and clients about what they expect moving forward in the relationship. It's a short and simple conversation that really helps build trust. Why? Because you demonstrate, in a genuine way, that you care about the future of the relationship and that you'll still be around long after a product is sold or a service is rendered.

There are many ways to enter into this sort of conversation. Here are a couple:

1. "If you could build the perfect _____ [insert your title here] _____, what would he or she look like?" or "what would be the person's characteristics?"

2. "Let's imagine it's three years from today and we've been working together for that time. How will you know we've been successful? What is your measure of the success of our relationship?"

Of course, there are many ways to enter into a conversation on expectations. You must use words that are genuine and natural for you. This is a conversation you want to have early in new relationships, possibly with a new prospect in the very first meeting. And it should be revisited from time to time throughout the relationship.

ARTICULATING YOUR VALUE
WITH CONFIDENCE BUILDS TRUST

How we speak to our prospects and clients about the work we do can definitely help us build trust more quickly. The keys are confidence and clarity. Most business owners, salespeople, and other professionals wing it when it comes to how they talk about their value. But if you want to build trust and credibility in your efforts to make sales, winging it may be significantly hurting you.

Let's say you were looking for a coach for your business and you decided to interview two or three candidates. And let's say you asked them questions such as, "How do you do what you do?" "For whom do you do what you do?" "Why do you do what you do?" and "What makes you different from other coaches?" I think you would choose (trust) the coach who was able to answer those questions clearly, confidently, and succinctly. Winging it does not build trust. Agree?

So can *you* answer those questions without hemming and hawing? Or do you have clear, short, confident answers? Anyone who takes the time to do the preparation to answer those questions will win more new clients. I guarantee it!

ACTION STEP

Over the next week, when you're speaking with small business owners, salespeople, or other professionals, ask them questions such as "What do you do?" "How do you do it?" "Whom do you do it for?" and "What makes you different?" Listen to their answers. Do those people have immediate, clear, confident, and sincere answers? Or do they hesitate? Now you know how you might be showing up to others if you haven't done your work in this area. Then work on your answers and practice delivering them.

NOT MAKING ASSUMPTIONS BUILDS TRUST

How many times in your life—with clients, coworkers, friends, and family—have you assumed something, only to find out you were wrong? I suspect many, many times. The bigger the incorrect assumption, the more trouble we get ourselves into.

Steven Gaffney is an author and expert in the area of honest communication. He has written three books on the topic, *Just Be Honest,*

Honesty Works, and *Honesty Sells* (http://www.StevenGaffney.com), and is an expert in "getting the unsaid, said." In all his work, he teaches a distinction he calls "Notice-Imagine." He makes a great case for the concept that what we "notice" or "the facts" of a situation make up about 10 percent of our communication and that what we "imagine" or "our assumptions" make up about 90 percent of our communication. Knowing this, we can now see how much we get it wrong and why we need to be aware of this dynamic.

Gaffney's solution to this potential problem is to "check it out." When a prospect or client says something that isn't completely clear to you, check it out. When you are listening to a prospect and taking notes, repeat back what you thought you heard. Whenever you sense you might be off base with something, check it out.

ADJUSTING TO PEOPLE'S COMMUNICATION STYLE BUILDS TRUST

How people communicate their message to you is how they best hear your words. If people are very direct in their style of communication, they usually trust others who are direct with them. But they don't trust (as easily) people who are much less direct in their style. Right or wrong, they perceive the indirect style as being "weak." And the reverse is true. If you are very direct, your direct style of communication can push away less direct people (and you might not even be aware of it).

Some people like to get down to business right away; they don't like small talk. Other people need to have a little small talk to warm up the conversation before they get to talking about business. Too much small talk will drive a task-oriented person nuts. Getting down to business with a relationship-oriented person too soon will seem cold and impersonal.

In a nutshell, most humans feel most comfortable with people who communicate like themselves. It seems to be human nature.

And, of course, most intelligent and mature adults have learned how to be flexible and broaden their field of play—to be more accepting and effective with people who are different from them. This is a good thing.

I see it this way. When we encounter people with a different communication style from ours, we give them the gift of our flexibility. In a sincere way, we adjust our style so they will feel more comfortable. We don't become a different person, inauthentic. We just move a little in their direction so they feel more comfortable and are more open to listening to what we say.

KNOWLEDGE AND EXPERTISE BUILD TRUST

With all this conversation about communication and relationship skills, I don't want to suggest that knowledge of products and services doesn't fit into the conversation about trust. It does!

Doing all the other things mentioned in this chapter on building trust, without becoming a true expert in one's field, will build "false trust." There's an illusion of trustworthiness with no foundation.

Learn how to explain even the most complicated aspects of what you do in terms that your prospects and clients can understand. Be very careful of using terms and jargon that are second nature to you but may not be to prospects. Teaching prospects and clients what they need to know will build trust, but it must be done in simple terms so they understand what you are saying and don't feel talked down to. Simple graphic illustrations should be used whenever possible to explain different aspects of your product or service.

Scientific studies have proved that most people learn faster and retain information longer when taken in through visual means over auditory means. Showing prospects and clients visual representations of concepts important to what you sell will aid their learning and retention and result in more sales for you.

NOT RUNNING FROM PROBLEMS
BUILDS TRUST

A relationship that's had a problem that's been handled well is a stronger relationship than one that's never had a problem. Agree? When problems hit, do you get a sinking feeling inside, or do you get energized about the opportunity? Okay, maybe that's a bit optimistic, but do you sincerely view problems as opportunities? And I'm not talking platitudes, here. I'm sincere when I say that I truly do believe that problems are opportunities.

Problems are opportunities to test yourself and show others what you're made of. Problems are opportunities to learn more about yourself and others—including your clients. Problems are opportunities to gain more expertise in your field. My friend Gary Glazer calls problems "jackpots" because they are opportunities to build stronger trust.

Not only do you not want to run from problems—becoming defensive and deflective—but you want to adopt the habit of digging for problems. You want to establish the habit of creating safe environments where your clients can complain, even about the least little things.

ACTION STEP

Tell your prospects early on in your sales process, "One thing you can count on from me is that I will not run away from problems. If we hit a snag, I'll be there for you. In fact, I will be checking in with you from time to time just to make sure our communication is candid and our relationship is on solid ground." Notice how the trust seems to build more quickly because of this.

ASKING THE RIGHT QUESTIONS

13

SELLING STARTS WITH GREAT QUESTIONS

To get prospects to give you time, let you ask them questions, and listen to your recommendations, they have to trust you and view you as a credible resource. Clearly, working from referrals contributes greatly to both those issues. There are other ways to build credibility as well. Relationship expert Andrew Sobel, author of *Power Questions: Build Relationships, Win New Business, and Influence Others* (John Wiley & Sons), makes the case that asking the right kinds of questions helps you build credibility in the eyes of your prospect. He says, "The questions we ask are often more important than what we *tell*. The CEO of a $12 billion company summed it up neatly when he told me, 'When someone walks into my office and is trying to market to me or sell something, I can always tell how experienced they are by the quality of the questions they ask.'"

You may already know the importance of asking the right questions. This chapter will address this important topic from several different directions, all designed to help you assess and adjust your questioning strategy.

ASK PERMISSION TO ASK

As we've already discussed, the questions you ask your prospects will go a long way in building credibility and value and will help you see if you have solutions to their problems. I've always maintained that the process of asking prospects questions should be a discussion, not an inquisition. You have to be careful how you present the questions you ask and how you break up those questions with other parts of your sales conversation.

Dirk Zeller, in *Telephone Sales for Dummies* (http://www .DirkZeller.com), recommends you "ask permission to ask." He says, "Before you jump into a deluge of questions, you want to ask the prospect if you can ask her some questions. Believe it or not, asking permission to ask questions is effective and shows the prospect that you respect her and her time. By allowing the prospect the choice of answering your questions, you frame the opening dialogue and launch it on a positive path."

Cindy, would it be okay if I ask you a few questions about your specific situation?

Cindy, before I make any recommendations of how I might be able to be a resource for you and your firm, I have a few critical questions I need to ask. May I proceed?

Cindy, what you just mentioned seems very important to what we're discussing here. May I probe a little further into that? I think your answers will be very helpful to this conversation.

THE RIGHT QUESTIONS
MOVE YOU TO THE SALE

Here's an exercise for you and your colleagues that will make you a lot of money, by getting to know exactly what you need to know about your prospects in order to make recommendations that will pique their interest:

1. Make a list of all the problems and challenges your prospects and clients face related closely and loosely to what you offer. Each one of these problems can yield one or more open or closed questions.

2. From this list you just made, go deeper by making a list of questions that look for the impact or implication of the problems and challenges. What's the problem? What's the impact of that problem—how is it impacting the prospects personally and their business? (Notice I said "personally *and* their business." Go for both.)

3. Make a list of all the benefits you deliver. Each one of your benefits can yield one or more open or closed questions. There may be some overlap between the problem questions and benefit questions.

4. Make a list of what you believe the "benefits of your benefits" (the positive effects of your benefits) to be. Each one of these may yield one or more questions you can ask.

This is not an inquisition, but this list becomes your template for things you want to learn before you call (from referral source or Internet), from the first call, and during all the subsequent appointments.

PAIN VERSUS PLEASURE

Most psychologists and scientists agree that the two main motivators of action are moving toward *pleasure* and moving away from *pain*. What is the more powerful motivator of the two? Fear! Moving away from or preventing pain. Personally, I think that when you are working with prospects, in your attempt to see if you might be a good resource for them, you should apply both motivators. The problem I see is that most salespeople, business owners, and professionals don't know how to leverage the pain motivator. They talk about features and benefits, but may be missing the most powerful thing that will get their prospects to take action—relief from their problem or protection against future problems.

When crafting the questions that make up a big part of your process, be sure to include questions that elicit what isn't working and then keep going to detect the implication of those problems. For example, a financial advisor might find out that a client isn't saving enough money for retirement and other purposes. That's the problem. But what's the implication of that problem? Working much longer than the client wants? Having lots of dreams that go unfunded? Going to the implication of the problem is what usually engages the emotions. Once prospects are engaged emotionally, they tend to start looking for solutions.

Many sales experts describe this as "going for the pain." I even heard one "expert" say in a speech, "Put that knife in and then twist it until the prospect can't stand it anymore and looks to you for the solution." Wow! That seems a little drastic to me. In fact, I suspect if someone did that to me, I'd run away as quickly as possible.

This pain-pleasure-problem-solution dynamic needs to be balanced. In addition to questions that uncover the problems (pain), you need to have questions that help the prospect see what's possible—the solution (pleasure). Sometimes the prospect even knows what the solution is, but is stuck in inertia and unable to do anything about it. Questions that help your clients create a vision for a better future are also very effective.

CLOSED-END AND OPEN-END QUESTIONS

You probably already know a little about the difference between closed-end and open-end questions. Lee Boyan, in his book *Successful*

Cold Call Selling (AMACOM), shares some great advice about these two types of questions. And even though Lee's book is focused on cold calling, his advice works for referral selling as well. Lee says,

> There are two types of questions you will want to consider using. Closed-end questions, sometimes called directive or fact-finding questions, are those that can be answered with a yes or no or simple statement of fact. It is a popular misconception that closed-end questions are only those that can be answered with a yes or no. Another part of the misconception is that all questions starting with "who," "what," "where," or "when" are open-end. Not so.
>
> Here are some examples of closed-end questions:
>
> - How many people do you employ?
> - Have you ever heard of our company?
> - What brand of product are you currently using?
> - When will you be receiving another shipment?
> - Who supervises this project?
> - Where is your head office located?
> - Does this sound reasonable to you?
>
> Open-end questions, sometimes called nondirective or feeling-finding questions, usually cannot be answered with a yes or no or a simple statement of fact. There is virtually no limit to the length of their answer, hence, open-end. Here are some examples:
>
> - How does this affect your business?
> - What is it you like about brand X?
> - What is it you don't like about brand X?
> - How do you feel about this?
> - Why is that important to you?
> - What directions will you be taking in this regard?

The Importance of Balance

In my seminars, I often have salespeople write out a list of questions they ask on three different categories of calls: (1) new prospects; (2) prospects called on before who are giving all or most of their business to a competitor, and (3) current customers. For several years I kept track of the kind of questions listed. Ninety-four percent were closed-end questions.

GO FROM "HERE" TO "THERE"

I think we're making a good case for the power of asking the right questions. Here's a method of asking questions that we have just adopted at Referral Coach International and have already seen results. Our prospects are opening up more to what they want and what's keeping them from getting it.

Bill Whitley, in his book *Art of the Rainmaker*, says,

> One of my favorite Power Questions is something I call the *here/there* question. Using a piece of paper, I say, "Let's say that you are *Here* and over the next few years you want to get *There*. There are certain things that will help you get *There* faster; let's call those things *Accelerators*. And of course my job—should we work together—is to help you get *There* as fast as possible. There are also things that will slow you down. Let's call them *Detractors*. My job is also to help reduce or eliminate these *Detractors*."
>
>   Then I ask my client four questions:
>
> 1. "Where is *There* for you?" *There* is simply the client's goal; the quest, the journey, the thing that they are trying to achieve related to the work you do. I let the client do most of the talking and I take notes as quickly and thoroughly as

possible. When I have a good picture of *There,* I summarize and synthesize what they have said. The six most powerful words you can use to start your summary are, "Here's what I heard you say . . ." When you listen intently and get it the first time, your prospect appreciates it and their faith in you begins to rise.

2. Once I have a good picture of *There*, I go backward and ask, "Where is *Here* for you?" I want to get a clear picture of their current situation. Again, I let them do most of the talking and I listen intently and summarize what I learn.

3. Once we have a good picture of *Here* and *There* I ask them, "What are the *Accelerators* that will help you get *There* faster?" I'm still listening, but I might suggest a couple of additional *Accelerators* based on my knowledge of their situation and other businesses.

4. The last question I pose is, "What are the *Detractors* that slow you down?" I'm always amazed at what I learn with this question. If you have done a good job of listening and summarizing on the first three questions, your client is more than willing to bear his soul and share intimate details of foibles, distractions and missteps. Be careful not to judge; simply listen, summarize and empathize.

CREATING AN EFFECTIVE SALES PROCESS

14

PROCESS-DRIVEN SALES

I sincerely believe that most small business owners, salespeople, and other professionals pretty much wing it when it comes to selling. They don't use a consistent, proven process to convert their prospects into clients. They have a few key questions they like to ask and a few key points they like to make, but very few think in terms of putting their prospects through a process.

As I keep saying, by working through referrals, every part of your sales process becomes easier to accomplish and more effective in producing results. Having a process will increase your confidence and make you more referable at the same time.

This chapter will give you the elements of a great sales process. You will need to take a little time to adopt these principles and tactics to your world. When you do, you will see an immediate increase in your results.

THINK PROCESS, NOT PRODUCTS

If you'd like to make sales *and* get referrals more quickly in your new relationships, then you need to think *process* over *products* (or services). You need to make the sale in such a way that the brand-new client wants to tell others about you.

And Your Process Is?

Do you have a clearly defined process through which you put most of your new clients? Do you help them think big picture? Do you educate them? Do you help them clarify their goals? Do you question their assumptions? Do you lead them to make the right decisions and stop procrastinating? Do they *grow* just a little by virtue of going through your process? Do you use the same process virtually every time, or do you wing it?

Take a minute to think about the process you put your prospects through from the minute you first contact them, all the way through to when they become a client and beyond. Are you creating "memorable experiences"? Is your initial process referable? How do you know if your process is referable? You're getting referrals without asking for them—just from your process—before your prospects even become clients! People are saying, "I have a colleague who should know about you" before you really deliver your product or service.

Leveraging Your Process

Here are five steps that will ensure you get the most out of your process—to make your clients happy and to generate word of mouth and referrals:

1. Have a clearly defined process that is repeatable and be clear on how your clients benefit.

2. Name your process. When you name your process, it becomes yours. No one else has your process. Prospects or clients can only get this process from you. This is a way to distinguish yourself in a crowded marketplace.

3. Illustrate your process with graphic design—on paper and your website. This brings your process to life. It helps you

explain your process to your clients and COIs. Visuals go into the mind faster and stay there longer.

4. Communicate to prospects, clients, and COIs why and how your process is beneficial. Get in the habit of talking about your process on a regular basis.

5. Bring your process to life with stories, anecdotes, and case studies.

So—if you want to become referable quickly in your new relationships and remain referable throughout—your mantra from now on is "process, not products." Work to make the sale, but do it in a way that brings such great value to your prospects and new clients that they want to tell others about you right away.

ACTION STEP

Take a long, hard look at your process for converting a prospect into a client. Is it merely designed to make the sale, or is it designed to bring value all along the way? The former will help you create sales. The latter will help you create more sales and be more referable more quickly.

BE TRANSPARENT WITH YOUR SALES PROCESS

Do you have a two-step, three-step, or four-step (or more) sales process? Do you even know? While it's always good to be able to be flexible in any situation, once you've found a sales process that works well for both you and your prospects, maintain consistency. And don't be afraid to let your clients know what your process is.

George, for us to determine if it makes sense for us to work together, I have a three-step process that seems to work well. First, we need to learn a little bit about each other. I need to learn about your situation to see if there are some ways I may become a resource for you. You probably want to learn about me and my firm so you'll know if you feel comfortable working with us.

Next, based on that conversation—if I truly believe I can help you—I will make some recommendations for you to consider.

Finally, we'll see if working together makes sense and what that looks like moving forward. How does this sound?

Obviously, this is a made-up conversation. But it gives you a feel for how you might lay out your process to the prospect. Now that you both know the process, it will be easier to stay on track, and when the time comes, your asking for the business is a natural next step.

Here are a few guidelines to keep your sales process moving forward:

1. When you describe your process to people in a prospect-centered manner, tell them that there are two primary reasons why multiple appointments make sense. First, you don't want to take up big chunks of their time. Second, after the first meeting, you're going to need a little time to digest the conversation and come back with meaningful suggestions.

2. At the end of your first appointment, you can make sure you have your second appointment scheduled. "Based on what we discussed today, I'll work up some suggestions we can discuss at our next meeting. I need about a week to get this prepared for you. Can we look at our calendars for late next week or early the following week?"

3. Find a few ways to be in touch with your prospects between meetings. This in-between-meetings contact can be related to your creating your proposal for them. It can consist of sending the summary notes of the last meeting or sending specific questions you have. It can be other pieces of evidence that will help them feel good about working with you. And it

can be articles or blog links or any type of information that you think your prospects will find useful. If you've created good rapport with your new prospects, you can also send information related to their hobbies, passions, and other personal interests.

SEVEN WORDS TO HELP YOU CLOSE MORE SALES

When you get on the phone with a prospect or a client—or meet in person—do you have a desired outcome for the call or meeting that is very clear? Clear intentions tend to produce clear results. Vague intentions tend to produce vague results.

For the rest of your career, *before* you get on the phone with a prospect or client . . . *before* you meet in person . . . think these seven words, "What's my desired outcome for this meeting?" (Or "phone call.")

Would you agree with me that when you have a clear desired outcome for a phone call or meeting, you're more likely to make that happen? The key word here is *clear*. Do you know exactly what you want your prospect or client to do as the result of your interaction? And if you do, do you create an agenda for the call or meeting that is likely to get you the result you desire? Do you craft the right questions that will get your prospect or client thinking in the ways you desire—and that are in the prospect's or client's best interest?

And as you formulate your goal for each call or meeting, always remain client focused. Always work for what's best for the prospect or client. When you do that, you'll get what you need.

ACTION STEP

From now on, never get on the phone or meet with a prospect without a clear goal of what you'd like to happen. Have a secondary goal, but first go for your primary goal.

TURN YOUR SELLING
INTO BRAINSTORMING

When you hear the word *brainstorm,* what comes to mind? Thinking of many ideas and not evaluating any one of them too quickly? The "P" part of my VIPS Method for asking for referrals is "permission to brainstorm." I believe the referral process should be collaborative with no pressure. There are no bad ideas!

What if you applied this same principle to other parts of your client acquisition process? That's what Dave, a business consultant in Tampa, Florida, does to perfection. He clears over $1 million in consulting fees each year.

Dave told me, "When I approach a new prospect, I tell them, 'I'm not here to sell you my consulting services. Think of our conversations as more of a brainstorming session. We're going to exchange a lot of ideas. We're going to ask each other a lot of questions. There are no bad ideas and no bad questions. Together, we're going to see if it makes sense for us to work together long term.'"

Dave said that his prospects love this approach because they understand the concept of brainstorming—collaboration without pressure. He said, "This approach frees me up to ask and say just about anything I want and the same is true for my prospect. This simple paradigm shift has won me more new business than I ever imagined and the 'brainstorming theme' continues into the consulting relationship, allowing us to do some very powerful work together."

FINDING THE DECISION MAKER

You probably already know that you always want to do your best to have the key decision maker actively involved in your selling process. Sometimes that's an easy thing, sometimes not. If you're selling to consumers, for instance, then it's often important to have both the husband and wife present at your appointments. Perhaps you've heard the term *one-legged appointment*? This is when you need to have the husband and wife present for your process but only one is there. This will often (though not always) cause the sale to take longer than necessary because the husband and wife have to consult with each other, usually with you not there to help in that consultation.

If you're working business to business, then there is often more than one decision maker involved. And sometimes it's a challenge to get in front of the key decision maker. Sometimes the person will use a subordinate as a shield. I run into this all the time.

Make it a habit of asking your contact, "In addition to yourself, who might also be involved in this decision?" When you get the answer, you say, "For the sake of efficiency and clear communication, the next time we talk [meet], can everyone involved be there?"

Sometimes a committee is the decision maker. What fun! When you send information to your contact, send enough packets for all the committee members to have in front of them.

I know some folks who just won't engage in the sales process if they can't have direct contact with the decision maker. I can certainly understand this perspective. And I suspect there are some businesses where this is a must. In many businesses, however, you can still work your process; it's just a little harder. I know that I've certainly acquired some very large accounts without ever speaking with the key decision maker. My contact was my "champion" in the company's process. When you can't speak directly to the key decision maker, then your reputation and body of evidence become even more critical players in your process.

PEST, PATHETIC, OR PERSISTENT?

How many times do you need to contact a prospect before that prospect agrees to do business with you? The answer is, "It depends." It depends on what you sell; products and services vary in their sales cycle. And it depends on where the prospects are in their awareness of their problem and willingness to make a change. Since this book is about contacting and meeting with prospects you acquired through a referral, let's remind ourselves of the three main reasons why prospects will meet with you from a referral:

1. The prospects know they need your product or service. They've just been waiting to meet someone they think they can trust.

2. The trust level between the referral source and the prospect is so high, that when the source says, "Take his call," the prospect says, "Okay!"

3. You have learned something from the referral source about the new prospect and have crafted a compelling reason why that prospect should meet with you.

While the first and second reasons are great when they are present, you certainly can't always count on them. In Chapter 6, on turning referrals into introductions, I suggested a great question to ask your referral source every time you get a referral: "What's going on in the referred person's life (or business) that's important to the person right now?" The answer to this question can be the very reason why that prospect should meet with you sooner than later.

But what if the prospect isn't ready to commit to a meeting? Or what if the prospect meets with you but isn't ready to take the next step in the relationship? If the prospect isn't an "A+" prospect, a successful veteran may elect to just move on. A less successful person or a rookie may want to stay in touch with that prospect. Sometimes timing really is everything.

Professional Persistence

Over the years I've heard many statistics on how many contacts a salesperson must make with a prospect before the sale is made. I've read five times, seven times, sometimes more. It really can depend on the complexity of your sale. While there are so many contributing factors to this, it's safe to say that your ability to be professionally persistent with certain prospects is a great skill to cultivate.

Some of my largest, most profitable clients have taken several years to land. I had to find ways to be appropriately proactive with them until the timing was right for them to do business with me.

Value-Centered Persistence

Early in my sales career, I would never give up on a prospect, but my contacts weren't always very purposeful. Looking back, I feel like some of my calls weren't more than, "Are you ready to buy yet?" I guess I had some success in spite of myself.

It finally dawned on me that I had to be value centered in my follow-up. Every time I called a prospect, I tried to bring something new to the conversation—something, I hoped, the prospect would find helpful.

As I've already discussed, in most sales scenarios, one battle in client acquisition efforts is inertia on the part of the prospects. Changing products or service providers is not always an easy proposition for clients. Sometimes the devil they know is better than the devil they don't know. Sometimes you really have to distinguish yourself in the eyes of the prospects before they will contemplate moving their business to you.

Of course, meeting them through a referral is one key way to distinguish yourself. Another way to do that is to keep providing them with value in the courtship process (and beyond).

People Buy What's Familiar

There's an old story about this soldier who went off to war and wrote his fiancée every day. For the first nine months, the soldier received almost as many letters in return as he wrote. Then the number began to dwindle. Not to be discouraged, the soldier kept writing every day. Soon, the letters from his fiancée stopped. When the soldier returned home, he found the love of his life married to the postman. People buy what's familiar!

Here are a few ideas for you to consider in your efforts to remain professionally persistent:

1. **Determine who qualifies.** You need to determine for yourself who is "worthy" of this professional persistence. The problem is that many don't have any guidelines about who merits this persistence and who doesn't, and way too often they stay in touch with lower-level prospects merely because they don't have enough top prospects in their pipeline.

2. **Build an inventory of value-centered materials.** Build an inventory of educational materials (printed and electronic) you can drip on your prospects. Of course, a newsletter should be a part of this inventory, but it's usually not nearly enough. Be on the lookout for articles—printed or electronic—that you think your prospects and clients might find interesting and helpful. These articles can be related specifically to your core product or service or can just be of general interest.

3. **Work on the personal side.** I always encourage people to build business friendships with their prospects and clients—to get to know each other in ways that go way beyond the business they do together. Don't be shy about allowing your personal interests to enter into even your prospecting relationships. I know one small business owner who owns two show dogs, and his prospects and clients are always asking him about how they are doing in their dog shows. In turn, get to know your prospects' interests and hobbies. When you see a newspaper or magazine article that relates to one or more of your prospects, send it out with a sticky note on it, saying, "Thought of you when I saw this."

It's a good idea to mix up how you stay in contact with your prospects. Use a combination of phone, e-mail, mail, and fax. You might even use a courier service from time to time for emphasis. But make sure you don't let all your prospecting relationships turn to low-touch methods such as mail and e-mail. There is no substitute for a telephone conversation or in-person meeting with a prospect.

ARE YOU WILLING TO
WALK AWAY FROM BUSINESS?

"Walking away from business"—now there's a concept that you don't often hear discussed. I think there are three main situations in which you should consider walking away from a potential new client.

Client Doesn't Fit Your Business Model

When you accept clients who don't fit your business model, you don't have as much time to attract and serve the clients who *do* fit your model. Why do people take clients who don't fit? Two main reasons: (1) they have a scarcity mentality, or (2) they are afraid to say no.

Be on the lookout for the *scarcity mentality*—meaning you see prospects and clients as a scarce resource and so you'll take anything that comes along. This often unconscious way of thinking or believing keeps many a talented person from reaching his or her full potential. The truth is, there are plenty of great clients out there; you just have to put yourself in the right flow.

Client Isn't Pleasant to Work With or Has
Unrealistic Expectations

I sincerely believe that an initial meeting between you and a prospect should be a mutual interview so that you both can see if you like each other and have similar expectations related to your product or service. How many times have you had a gut feeling, "I don't think I'm going to enjoy working with this person," and you bring the person on as a client anyway? Trust your gut! It will save you time, aggravation, and often money in the long run.

Client Is Stringing You Along

Have you noticed that many prospects don't know how to say no to you? Sure, many of them have no trouble at all, but many others give you noes disguised as "maybes." At some point, you go for the no. You say to this prospect who keeps telling you to call back in three months, "George, I've appreciated your willingness to stay in touch. I get the feeling that you're being very polite, but the prospects of us working together aren't that strong. Is that a fair statement?"

When you say this to prospects—especially if they know they've been stringing you along—you're likely to get one of two responses. They might say, "Well, I guess you're right. I am very happy with my current advisor." Whew! Now you can stop wasting your psychic energy on them as a prospect. (This, by the way, doesn't mean you stop dripping on them in some soft way—especially if they are a big fish—but now you know the score.)

The second response could be, "No, no. I really am interested. It's truly a matter of timing. Let me explain a little better . . ." Now you know you still have a decent prospect.

In the long run, your willingness to walk away from imperfect situations will help you build a stronger business that will also produce more referrals.

TALKING ABOUT YOUR VALUE

15

TALKING ABOUT YOUR BUSINESS

One of the beauties of the referral process—particularly when you get introduced—is that many of your new prospects will already have a sense of your business and the value you provide.

How you talk about your business (your value proposition)—the words you use and the conviction behind those words—is a critical step in converting referral prospects into new clients. The questions you ask will help you tailor your remarks to your prospects. And learning how to articulate your value proposition is never a one-time process. This is something that demands constant tweaking and occasional overhaul.

This chapter gives you strategies and tactics to talk about your business (products or services) in a way that will pique intellectual and emotional interest—moving your prospects to take action.

ENTHUSIASM AND BELIEF

Someone once told me, "When you leave the room, the enthusiasm should remain." I think that letting your enthusiasm for what you sell show through will help you bring in more new clients. Enthusiasm is contagious. When your referral source recommends you enthusiastically and your prospect senses your enthusiasm, it's a winning combination.

Now, by enthusiasm, I don't mean *jumping-up-and-down excited*. It's just a conviction and confidence that emanates from you. You need to match how you express your enthusiasm for what you do with the personality of your prospect. If she has an open personality, if she is someone who shows her enthusiasm for ideas readily, then perhaps you can wear your enthusiasm on your sleeve. This won't bother her. In fact, she may feed on it. On the other hand, if you are with a more guarded person, you better pull back on how much excitement you show. Show confidence and conviction but remain on a very even keel. Too much enthusiasm can push guarded people away.

What's Even More Effective Than Enthusiasm?

Belief! Like enthusiasm, belief is transferable. But belief goes deeper than enthusiasm. If you believe in what you sell, then your clients will pick up on that. It's a contagious and attractive quality. If you don't believe it, then certainly don't expect them to.

If you are trying to sell something that you don't really believe in, then your success will always be limited by that belief. I think you can even use the word *belief* or *believe* when you are talking to prospects.

> *George, as you can probably tell, I'm very enthusiastic about the work we do and how it will help you transform your business. My enthusiasm comes from a strong belief in our process and the tangible results we've helped other firms just like yours produce. We have literally hundreds of clients who have endorsed our work. My enthusiasm and belief come from the results. I'm hoping we will have the opportunity to help you in the same way. What do you think about moving forward at this time?*

Do you believe in what you do? How are you making sure that belief shows through? Do you need to craft a few sentences (like the example above) and add them to your sales process?

FROM ENTHUSIASM AND
BELIEF INTO TRUE CONVICTION

Sometimes, first starting out in your business, you're not fully aware of the true value of the work you do. Therefore, it's often hard to display the proper belief and enthusiasm. It's usually an evolutionary process.

For example, when I first got started in the referral business, I was more of a generic sales expert. I had some good ideas that people found helpful, but I wanted to narrow my focus to expand my results. I knew the power of becoming a "specialist." So I wrote my first book on referrals, which hit the market in 1996. As I began teaching my strategies, I knew that they worked for me, but I wasn't 100 percent certain that they would work for others—that they would be fully transferable to other salespeople, business owners, and professionals across various industries.

As I spoke to groups and wrote my newsletter, I always had a nagging feeling that maybe what I was sharing wasn't that valuable to others. I certainly had a gap in my enthusiasm and belief in the work I was doing. Can you relate to this dynamic?

Then the feedback started coming in. And, luckily, I paid attention to it and took it in. People started writing me notes telling me about the results they had produced with some of my ideas. Slowly, the body of evidence gained quite a bit of momentum. I received more and more requests to speak on the topic of referrals. I started putting together video-based training programs and started writing my next book, *Get More Referrals Now!*

I went from a place of cautious enthusiasm and belief, to a place of great conviction in the work that I do. Here's the important thing: as I was able to convey that conviction to my prospects, everything expanded for me. My prospects felt my conviction and wanted to work with me. And as I delivered speeches and seminars, I saw the attendees get lit up by that conviction.

Not to brag (okay, nothing wrong with a little self-promotion every now and then), but in the middle of writing this book, I spoke by phone with a client whom I was debriefing on a pilot program I had just conducted for his firm. The results were undeniable. But he said something to me that sums up this section. He said, "Bill, while the results are better than we expected, one of the reasons we want to roll this out to all 2,500 reps across the country is because you got them fired up about referrals in a way we just couldn't do with our in-house training program. We see that your depth of knowledge, along with your incredible enthusiasm and belief in your system, has made all the difference."

Wow! The power of conviction! People notice it and they want more.

WHAT MAKES YOU DIFFERENT?

I don't have to tell you that being able to differentiate yourself from your competition is critical to maximizing your success. Yet in response to the question of what makes you different, most small business owners, salespeople, and other professionals struggle to come up with an answer that truly means something to their prospects.

Here are a few thoughts to help you figure this out and formulate a way you can express this to prospects, clients, and COIs.

What Do Your Clients Say?

Whenever you are crafting answers to the question of what makes you different, go to your clients. Ask them what makes you different in their eyes. Why do they do business with you? Why did they choose you over someone else? Why do they stay with you? What do they say to their colleagues about you? When you ask your clients these types of questions, two things happen. One is that you learn things you wouldn't have thought of yourself. The other is that what you learn is expressed in what I like to call "client speak," meaning words that are in clients' heads; when you use client speak with prospects like them, the prospects will *get it* right away.

What Makes You Relevant?

Sometimes shifting the question just a bit will trigger new ideas for you. Instead of "What makes you different?" answer the question "What makes you relevant?"—in today's world, in your marketplace, to your prospects and clients?

If you expect prospects to even consider what you have to offer, especially if they're already working with someone similar to you, then you have to have the answers to these questions. Even if your prospects don't ask you what makes you different, I can guarantee they're thinking it. So make sure you insert the answer into your conversations with prospects.

In addition to helping you secure appointments and new business with clients, how you talk about the work you do will also help your prospects and current clients talk about you to others. They often get their cues from you. So there's a direct relationship between how you talk about your value proposition and how others talk about your value proposition.

A POWERFUL WAY TO DIFFERENTIATE YOURSELF

One thing I've learned is that of all the things you discuss with your prospects, one of the most powerful is to tell them *why* you do what you do.

Science has proved that people make buying decisions with the emotional side of their brain. Logic and reason certainly play a part, but at the end of the day they need to *feel good* about their decision. So as you ask your prospects good probing questions and then talk about the work you do, you want to make sure that you hit the emotional side of their brain in a positive way.

Talk about your *why*. Here are places to look for your *why*.

- Why did you get started in this business in the first place?

- Why are you still in the business you're in?

- Why are you excited about your product or service?

- Why do you work for the firm you do?

- Why is it an exciting time for you and your business?

Here's an example using my *why*:

Let me tell you a little about why I'm in this business. I've found that most businesspeople serve their clients well, but they don't know how to fully leverage their great service and client relationships. There's a gap between where they are and where they'd like to be in terms of acquiring more high-value clients through referrals and other relationship marketing strategies. I derive a lot of pleasure from opening up people's eyes to what's possible and then giving them the tools to make it happen. I'm in the business of closing that gap, and I love it when my clients come back to me to report their great results. I'm hoping I can do the same for you and have you thanking me as well.

Of course, your words will be different, but you can see how this can bring your passion and belief in what you do into the conversation. When you talk about your *why*, you will feel the energy in the room (and even over the phone) change. People will listen to you a little differently because you're hitting them in a different part of their brain.

ACTION STEP

Determine your why. Craft a way to talk about it. Practice saying it a few times. Start to use it. And don't wait for someone to ask you, "Why do you do what you do?" Introduce it into the conversation yourself.

SELL THE "BENEFITS OF THE BENEFITS"

Pay attention to this next idea. This idea has helped me transform how I talk about my business. Sales trainer and author John Palumbo (http://www.JohnPalumbo.com) shared this concept with me recently. How can you apply it to your business? "Most salespeople have been taught classic *feature and benefit* selling. For example, you probably know that if you want to sell someone a computer, just doing a *feature dump*—obsessing over things like increased processor speed, a low-glare screen, and wireless connectivity—won't close the sale. You've got to engage in a meaningful discussion about the benefits of these features.

"Does the processing speed make it easier for the user to save and send files that contain lots of graphics? Is the screen easier to read when working outdoors? Does the wireless-connectivity software automatically connect with available networks, so less time is spent troubleshooting connections and inserting passwords? This is how good salespeople transition from features to benefits.

"But *Master Closers* don't stop there. They take the conversation to the next level by selling benefits of the benefits. For example, a feature of a smart phone might be its ability to run word processing and presentation programs. A benefit of this feature might be the phone's ability to help a prospect update client documents more quickly. Once you've established how a feature benefits the prospect, you're not done. Ask the prospect about the benefits of the benefit. In our example, you should find out directly from the prospect how the benefit of quicker updating of client documents would be beneficial.

"Maybe this benefit would help the prospect generate greater revenue, improved client loyalty, and more referrals. You may not know exactly what the benefits of the benefit will be until you actually have the discussion with the prospect. Once you do have that discussion, however, you will have begun the process of shared visualization that *Master Closers* use to win sales.

"When meaningful benefits are discussed out loud, prospects always experience an emotional response. Your job is to notice that response and dig deeper. Ask your prospect what the benefits of your product or service mean to them. In our particular example you might say, 'How would the ability to deliver edited files to clients and prospects faster than your competition benefit you and your business?' Continue questioning your prospect until you both share a vivid mental picture of what that benefit will look like and how it will feel. Then use these mental images to build excitement and close the sale."

Never assume your prospect knows the benefits of what you offer. Sales expert Lee Boyan says, "Benefits are not inherent in the product or service being sold. Benefits are in the prospect's mind. If they are not in the prospect's mind at the moment you approach, you must put them there or they will not exist for the prospect at that particular moment. Features can exist without the prospect, but the benefits can't."

Art Sobczak puts it this way, "People buy because they picture themselves already enjoying the results of your product or service."

I like John's, Lee's, and Art's thinking here. We often talk about features and benefits as *we* see them, but do we go to the next step and ask our prospects how *they* see them impacting their life and business? That's the "benefit of the benefit."

ACTION STEP

Create three columns on a piece of paper or word processing document. Column 1 is for product or service *features*. Column 2 is for the *benefits* of those features. You may have already done this

exercise a dozen times. Now, as John says, go the next step. In
column 3, specify how you would ask your prospect to elaborate
on the *benefit of the benefit*. What words would you use? Giving
some thought to what your prospects might say will help you in
crafting these questions.

BENEFITS OR TRANSFORMATIONS?

Lately, I've shifted from talking about benefits to talking about transformations. Perhaps it's an argument of semantics, but what do people
really want? They want to transform their situation. You're reading
this book because of the possibility of transforming (increasing) your
sales production through referrals.

I often talk about taking people from point D to point T. What do I
mean by that? Point D is "dabbling in referrals." Point T is a "thriving,
referral-based business." That's the transformation I strive to provide
to everyone with whom I work. The benefit of the benefit, as described
in the previous strategy, is often the transformation people seek.

What transformations do you provide to your clients? From where
to where do you take them? Talk about where they are now and where
they can be. That's transformation. List your benefits and then see
what your ultimate one or two transformations are. Start talking
about the transformations you help your clients with. You'll see how
they respond just a little better and with more interest.

ARE YOU USING YOUR
CLIENT ATTRACTION STORY?

Bill Whitley, in his book *Art of the Rainmaker*, teaches a great strategy
he calls "Your Client Attraction Story." Since all buying decisions are
made from the emotional part of the brain, and stories impact that

part of the brain, a Client Attraction Story is a very powerful tool that you should use in just about every sales scenario.

Here is an excerpt from *Art of the Rainmaker* that explains what goes into your Client Attraction Story . . .

Five Parts of Your Client Attraction Story

Everyone loves a great story. That's why we enjoy movies, books and TV. The classic story format has five main parts. Think back to the stories and fairy tales you were told as a child. When your parents or grandparents read you a bedtime story I'm sure they sounded something like this:

1. Once upon a time there was a hero

2. Who had a reason to go on a journey

3. Where he/she/it met a huge challenge

4. To which there was a hero-inspired way out

5. And they all lived happily ever after

Client Attraction Stories (CAS) have the same five key parts. Let's take a look:

1. Once upon a time there was a hero . . . In a CAS one of your clients is always the hero. This is where you introduce that client and provide a little information about their situation.

2. Who had a reason to go on a journey . . . In a CAS, the journey is simply the goal that client wanted to achieve. It's the quest—that one elusive thing they were trying to achieve.

3. Where he met a huge challenge . . . The client ran into an obstacle (the problem that needed solving). No matter how hard he tried, something always held him back.

4. To which there was a hero-inspired way out . . . With your help the client overcame the obstacle. This is the most

important part of the story. Identify what steps the client took to overcome the obstacle and how you helped in the process. This is where the learning takes place. The obstacle would have been insurmountable had the client not taken the right action (with you involved in that, of course).

5. And he lived happily ever after . . . Thanks to the solution you helped the client implement, his life changed for the better. It usually involves increased revenue, increased profit, an efficiency gain, or prevention of a problem.

Story Themes

Some people find that it works better if they have more than one Client Attraction Story in their arsenal. Having several stories memorized, perfected and at their fingertips ensures that they have a story to fit any circumstance that they encounter. Five themes behind the Client Attraction Stories:

1. Why me: Focus on your integrity, commitment and follow-through.

2. Growth: Focus on increased revenue and market share.

3. Efficiency: Focus on increasing profit and saving time and money.

4. Buy right: Focus on making the right decision and offering good advice.

5. Protection: Focus on preventing problems.

ACTION STEP

It's time for you to craft one or more Client Attraction Stories you can introduce into your conversations with your prospects. Think of all the results you've helped your past and current clients achieve.

Apply the story formula to these case studies. Then work on telling a succinct but compelling story. Create more than one so you have different stories to fit different sales scenarios. Just like your why does, a Client Attraction Story hits the buying side of the brain and moves your prospects to like you, trust you, and want to do business with you.

THE MONEY CONVERSATION

While your price or fee is not the only thing your prospects take into consideration when thinking about working with you, it's always a factor. And working through referrals usually relieves some of the price pressure. Do you ever struggle with quoting your fees or get a lot of price resistance? This is a common challenge for many business-people. Here are a couple of strategies I've been using for quite some time that have helped me make more sales and have taken pressure off my fees and prices. I call it the "money conversation." Sales trainer Brian Sullivan (http://www.PreciseSelling.com) calls it being a more effective "financial presenter."

Let's See If This Makes Financial Sense

I got this from Brian Sullivan, and it really helps me get into the money conversation with ease and effectiveness. As I see that my prospect is forthcoming with information and is asking me questions that show genuine interest, I know it is time to talk money. I don't like to talk about money in the first few minutes of the conversation. I know I need to build the client's perceived need for the solutions I provide. I also know that, at some point, if we're not in the same financial ball park, there's no point in even playing the game.

So I'll say, "George, it sounds like you have some interest in what we offer, but I know you need to make sure it makes *financial sense*. I have a few questions that I think will help both of us see if the economics are going to work for you in this important decision. Can we go down that path at this time?" In my case, I have to help prospects determine if what they invest in our referral programs or training tools will deliver a significant return on their investment. The good news for me is that it always does, but I need their help in helping them see this for themselves. This strategy is the perfect way to enter into this money conversation.

Are We in the Ball Park?

Sometimes prospects will tell you their budget right away. Many won't. They are usually afraid you are going to come back with a proposal that fills up their budget just because they told you that amount. When I have prospects who are reluctant to tell me their budget or aren't clear on their budget, I give them some ball-park pricing to test the waters, therefore allowing me to work on a proposal that is more likely to be accepted.

Here's a sample conversation that brings this concept to life:

ME: *George, for me to prepare a proposal for you for a program that will create a great return on your investment, I need to have a sense of what you're willing to invest. Giving me a ball-park amount will help me determine (1) if we can we help you accomplish your goals and (2) how we can go about implementing your training program. Can you give me a sense of your budget?*

PROSPECT GEORGE: *I don't really have a budget at this time. Why don't you show me something, and we'll proceed from there.*

ME: *I'd be happy to show you some templates of how we can help you increase revenues by acquiring more clients through referrals. But I don't want to come in with a plan that doesn't even come close to making economic sense. We have three basic levels of programs. They range from about $3,000 to $40,000. As I craft a proposal for you, can you give me a range to stay within?*

PROSPECT GEORGE: *Well, I know we won't be able to go over $10,000, so can you present me with something that will work and that falls in that range?*

Now, I may still present other options with more value at the higher price range, but I'll lead with the option in the range my prospect has provided.

Chevy-Buick-Cadillac

Here's a method I've used for years. (Fees given below are purely fictitious.)

George, before I work up an action plan, it would help both of us if I had a handle on your budget for taking care of this issue. Let me put it in terms of three levels of solutions, each one being more comprehensive than the next.

Our "Chevy" solution is the most basic. It's possible it will be all you need to fix the problem, and the fee for that solution usually runs between $5,000 and $10,000.

Our "Buick" solution is more comprehensive and usually runs in the range of $10,000 to $20,000.

And our "Cadillac" solution is the most comprehensive—and the most popular I might add. For your situation, I expect this to run in the neighborhood of $40,000.

Brian Sullivan makes an important point about quoting your price or fee: "As you present your price or fee, don't change your body language or tone of voice. If you show reluctance, hesitation, or any sign of a lack of confidence, your prospect will detect this. It could break trust or cause your prospect to go for a lower price."

Take a look at how you are talking about money in your conversations with prospects. Are you willing to address it head on—over the phone or in person—or do you take the wimpy approach and always have to lead with it in writing? Can you apply this strategy of creating a ball-park range of the client's budget so you know if it's still worth pursuing the sale and you come in with the right plan and pricing?

BOURBON CHICKEN?

Just about every mall in the United States has a food court with a Chinese food vendor. If you get anywhere within about 20 feet of it, you will run into one of the vendor's employees holding out a piece of chicken on a toothpick and saying, "Bourbon chicken?"—meaning, "Taste this, you'll like this, and don't you want to buy this bourbon chicken?" Invariably I'll taste the sample and say to myself, "That'll do."

The *free sample* is an age-old marketing strategy. It's probably been around as long as people have been selling things. How can you use this strategy in your business?

At Referral Coach International, we have a free e-mail news-letter (http://www.ReferralMinute.com) and are always offering free reports, webinars, and many other tools that bring value to our prospects and clients. We know that when people *taste* what we have to offer, many will want more and will buy from us.

Ramon is a financial advisor on Long Island, New York. He was trying to earn the trust of a CPA so that she would refer some of her clients to him. This courtship went on for almost two years. Finally Ramon told the CPA, "I'd like to put you through the process I put my clients through. I don't want you to become a client. You may even beg me to work with you afterward, but that's not going to happen. I only want you to experience the value I bring to people so you will feel comfortable introducing your clients to me when the time is right for them."

The CPA agreed. Ramon put her through his process. She loved it. She begged him to become her financial advisor. He relented. He received seven referrals from her in the next four months.

TEACH THEM HOW TO BUY WHAT YOU SELL

When you have a prospect in front of you, one powerful strategy is to teach that prospect how to buy what you sell. Here are a couple of examples:

A friend of mine, Dave, owns a very successful roofing company. He told me that his business really took off when he stopped trying to sell roofs. This confused me a bit, so I asked him to explain.

"We used to go to the home, measure the roof, work up an estimate, hand it to the homeowner, and say, 'We'd love to do your roof for you.' We sold some roofs. Now, we go to the home, do all those same things, and then say, 'Whether you go with us or another company, your goal is to get a good roof at a fair price, correct?' (Yes) 'So whomever you choose, make sure that they give you heavy-gauge flashing and that they use a proper nail pattern—some roofers out of ignorance or haste don't nail the roof down properly." He goes on to teach them how to buy a roof.

Does this concept apply to you? You bet it does!

Let's say you're shopping for a new mattress. One salesperson says, "Lie down on a few and pick the one that feels most comfortable. That's the one for you." Another one says, "Let me show you the differences in mattresses and what makes them different—why some cost more than others. You'll need to try them out, but I want you to understand why one mattress may feel better to you than another." Which person are you going to buy from? The one who *teaches* you! You may even pay a little more to do business with this person.

ACTION STEP

Make sure you have five to seven teaching points (or more) that educate your prospects so they can make an informed decision. Set your points down in writing. Go through them at your meeting (or send them in advance to help you secure the appointment). You will earn trust, and you will differentiate yourself from your competition.

A CONFUSED MIND NEVER BUYS

When's the last time you went shopping for a flat-screen TV? If you went to a store like Best Buy or HH Gregg, you probably saw a wall of

TVs from every major manufacturer and every current technology. If you didn't research exactly what you wanted, then you were probably a little overwhelmed. If you were lucky enough to find a sales assistant who knew what he was talking about, you finally came to a decision— all the while wondering if there was a better choice for you. If you didn't get the help you needed, you walked out. Can you relate?

One simple truth of sales and marketing is, "A confused mind doesn't buy." Having many choices is *not* always a good thing. At one point my company had too many referral tools in our online referral store. We knew that this was confusing people. We took off many of the tools or bundled them into special kits and sales went up.

Be extremely careful of offering too many choices to your prospects. As a general rule, offer no more than three choices at any one time. Sometimes two is even better. If you sense hesitation or indecision on the part of your prospects, it could be that you overwhelmed them with information and choices.

Perhaps you should say, "I know I've thrown a lot at you; let me simplify this a little," or "I know there are a lot of options; let's go through each one and simplify the process as we go." Then, if you feel you've learned enough about their situation and problems, and believe you have a good answer, you can recommend what you believe to be the "best option" or what you think "will work the best."

Assess the choices you give your prospects. Are you giving them too many options? Consider using a chart like software manufacturers do: "with A you get this; with B you get this; with C you get this." Presenting your choices in a visual manner is often very helpful to your prospects.

DEALING EFFECTIVELY WITH OBJECTIONS

16

DEFUSE OBJECTIONS

If you follow everything in this book up until this point, you will clearly reduce objections but never eliminate them. Sometimes you reach prospects at a bad time. Sometimes the introduction didn't create enough value to pique their interest. Sometimes you get their knee-jerk reaction to someone "who's trying to sell me something." Sometimes you run into impolite people. Sometimes you didn't ask the right questions or create enough value.

Some sales trainers will try to teach you to *overcome* objections. I think this strategy can be dangerous. If your goal is just to try to convince people that their thinking is wrong, they will often dig their heels in deeper. In doing research for this book, I read more than one expert saying, "Objections are simply a request for more information." Hogwash! Sometimes all the information in the world won't create interest or action.

The most important tool in diffusing objections is *understanding* the objections—sometimes before you even meet with your prospect. This chapter contains proven strategies to help you understand and diffuse your objections.

NEWTON'S FIRST LAW OF MOTION

Newton's first law of motion states: "An object at rest stays at rest and an object in motion stays in motion unless acted upon by an outside force." This means that there is a natural tendency of objects to keep on doing what they're doing. All objects resist changes in their state of motion. In the absence of an outside force, an object in motion will maintain its state of motion. This is often referred to as the "law of inertia." And inertia can play a huge role in your attempts to move prospects to take action.

Brian Tracy, in his book *The Art of Closing the Sale* (Thomas Nelson), says, "Another major obstacle to closing is *human inertia*. If a person is comfortable using a particular product or service, it is much easier for him to continue with what he is doing than to make a change. People get into a comfort zone. They become accustomed to their current methods. You may have a cheaper or better product, but the advantages and benefits you offer are often not enough to get the prospect to change his existing way of doing things."

I believe that to get a prospect to change from one product or service to another, from one way of doing things to a different way, you have to *disturb* the status quo in some way. You have to become that *outside force* for a new perspective and new action. If this seems to be a prevalent dynamic with most of your prospects—your prospects seemingly stuck with their current situations—don't avoid it. Bring it up early in your conversations. Just like any other objection, face it head on.

Here's one way you might address this dynamic with your prospects, sometimes from the very beginning of the relationship:

George, I know that making a change can often be difficult. Even when things aren't working exactly as you'd like, making a change takes an extra level of energy and courage. I liken it to Newton's first law of motion, which deals with inertia. Essentially, something will stay the same, remain on its current path, unless impacted by an outside force. Consider me that outside force to help you take a critical look at your situation, make a few recommendations if I see places for improvement, and then—if everything makes sense to you—help you manage that process of change.

DEALING WITH NO

Nick Murray, author of *The Game of Numbers,* says, "The two physical laws of prospecting: (1) 'Yes' is only potentially available at the risk of 'no.' And, therefore, (2) any activity/behavior to which another human being might respond by directly saying 'no' to you is a valid prospecting behavior."

There may be nothing more powerful in stopping you from taking any type of proactive sales action than the fear of getting a no. The fear of rejection is a powerful demotivator.

Anticipate the No

One of the most effective ways to reduce the fear of rejection is to be fully prepared for the no. In fact, I suggest you think of all the places you are likely to hear the word *no* (in all its forms) and then be prepared for that rejection.

While you should go into every conversation with positive expectations—expecting your ideas to be accepted—you must be prepared for the rejection so that it doesn't surprise you and throw you off.

It's Not Just the Rebuttal

Being prepared for the no is not just about having a clever rebuttal. Merely rebutting an objection can often backfire by making prospects or clients become more entrenched. A big confidence booster is understanding the reason for the no—understanding the "why" behind the objection.

The first response to any objection should be genuine curiosity, a genuine interest in learning more about the objection. Sometimes a simple "Tell me more" will get you to a deeper and more helpful level.

Bring Up the No

If you find that in your day-to-day prospecting and selling you get recurring objections, find ways to bring up the objections before your prospects or clients do. When a prospect stops the progress of your process with an objection, it can often create tension and cause you to lose focus or confidence.

On the other hand, when you bring up the objection, you remain in control (or relative control) of the conversation.

Long ago, I sold printing. I used to have fun cold-calling buyers of printing by saying, "Hi, this is Bill Cates with Thunder Hill Printing. My guess is you get a lot of calls from people trying to sell you printing." ("You got that right!") "Am I the first or tenth person to call you today?" ("Well, you're the first on today.") "I'm curious, what do you tell the others?"

By having fun and hitting my most common objection, I get people to warm up to my call. I have now earned a few minutes of their time to distinguish myself and spark their interest in wanting to meet with me.

> *George, as I go through this process, you may get the feeling that you want to think about my recommendations. And I certainly understand that. This is important work we're doing here and deserves careful consideration. If that thought comes to you, let me know. Given my experience, I can probably help you brainstorm a bit—to gain more clarity.*

Since I work from referrals, most of the prospects I speak to either call me or are open to the first conversation because their colleague told them it would be worth their time. I hope that this dynamic is true or becoming true for you as you become more adept with generating referrals and introductions. With that said, not every one of my prospects is ready to move forward with the exploratory process—mostly because of timing. They don't want to take on a training initiative until they are ready to support it full force.

This is a good perspective on their part. So I often say to prospects early in my first conversation, "I know that if you decide to move forward with a referral training initiative, the timing has to be just right, so that the training can be delivered and supported in the best way. Can we talk a little about the timing of such a project?" Now, instead of getting the objection "The timing isn't right for us right now," I purposely get into a conversation of the timing. I hit it head on. In this conversation about timing, I make sure that we discuss some of the results they will see from the training—so the prospects often get excited about the opportunities and decide to get started more quickly than they had originally thought. There have been times when this conversation has actually delayed clients using me. However, this is what was in the best interests of the clients. By waiting for the right time for them, they were able to maximize their investment in what we offer.

Alan Rigg, author of *How to Beat the 80/20 Rule in Sales Team Performance: A Step-by-Step Guide to Building and Managing Top-Performing Sales Teams* (http://www.8020salesperformance.com), writes, "Although no one wants to go in to a sales meeting expecting objections, this mindset is actually the best way to close the sale. Preparing a thoughtful response to any and all objections will help you to confidently guide your prospect toward making the deal."

Go for the No

As salespeople, we often get noes disguised as maybes. When you think a prospect or client is trying to tell you no in a very indirect manner, go for the no. "George, you said you were comfortable providing me with some introductions to your friends and colleagues, but

I'm getting the feeling you may be having second thoughts. Is that the case? If so, let's think through this for a minute." Assuming a maybe is a yes can lead to the client feeling pressured. Gaining clarity is always the best course of action.

Training for the No

If you are a sales manager or are responsible for the selling success of others, I suggest that you schedule regular "training sessions" designed to help all your reps get more comfortable, confident, and effective in dealing with no. Host a monthly "No Clinic" where you brainstorm the best ways to explore and reframe the various noes you get.

Delineate every area of your process where you might hear no. With the most common noes, think of ways to head these off at the pass, as described above.

Clarity and practice build confidence. Confidence generates courage and more effective action. This sort of ongoing training and awareness building will have a direct impact on your sales production.

ACTION STEP

Identify any reoccurring objections; this is best done with your sales team or colleagues (if possible). Figure a way to bring each of the objections up before your prospects do, so you can have a more complete discussion of it. Now you, rather than your prospects, have control of when that objection gets expressed. This will allow you to handle that objection more on your terms. Doing this is not meant to be tricky or manipulative—it's merely bringing up the truth and not trying to avoid it. Then practice this! Just talking about it may not give you the confidence you need to actually do it.

ASKING FOR
THE BUSINESS

17

ASK FOR THE BUSINESS

"You must ask for the business!" How many times have you heard that admonition? Plenty of times, I'm sure. So are you doing it? At some point in your process of attempting to turn a prospect into a client, are you asking the prospect to become a client? Are you asking the prospect to take action?

In the introduction to this section, I shared my philosophy on sales—that selling is simply a series of seeking permissions: permission to ask questions, permission to probe further, permission to keep the process moving to the next logical step. Well, one could say this is the "ultimate permission." You're seeking permission to confirm the new relationship.

I personally use every idea in this chapter. Am I perfect at it? Of course not, but I'm making constant improvement. Take this chapter to heart. Without using the ideas in this chapter, you will likely be missing many opportunities to confirm sales.

USE FORESHADOWING

Foreshadowing is a cinematic technique used in just about every movie to allow the movie to make sense all along the way. A character, weapon, or location at one point in the movie shows up again later to help the plot make sense. We can apply this technique of foreshadowing in many ways as we sell and service our clients.

For instance, there are many factors that play a part in converting a prospect into a client. One of these factors is, of course, asking for the business. There are many old-style "tricky" ways to try to convert a prospect into a client. I don't believe in tricky methods. I believe in being straight, but not aggressive, by using the technique of foreshadowing.

Some people even like to lay out those steps on the first appointment—*foreshadowing* the asking for the business. "Here's how I see us proceeding. First we'll get together to learn more about each other. One of my goals will be to bring you as much value as I can, so you will at least consider me as a resource. At some point, after we've learned enough and our questions are answered, we'll see if it makes sense to work together. How does that sound?"

I'm not saying you use those exact words. It illustrates one of many ways foreshadowing the next steps can play out and also be helpful in gaining commitment.

Then, when it's time to ask for the business—when it's time for you to suggest that you begin working together—you can say something like, "George, I think we're at that time for me to see if you're ready to go to the next step, namely, get this project under way."

Your words need to be genuine for you and fit your business circumstances. But using the technique of foreshadowing to ask for the business will give you confidence to do so and not surprise your prospect.

ALWAYS MAKE A RECOMMENDATION

I cannot tell you how many people I've seen present their ideas to prospects and then sit back wishing and hoping (and praying) the prospect will say, "Okay! Let's move forward." We must develop the habit of *asking* them to move forward. *How* you ask them to do this can make a big difference in your results.

Personally, I almost always like to make a recommendation. I say things like, "Here's what I recommend." "Here's how I recommend we move forward." "If I may be so bold, I'd like to recommend what I believe will be the best solution [choice] for you."

If you feel a need to be softer (working with a more indirect personality), then you can change *recommend* to *suggest*. *Suggest* is fine. *Recommend* has more conviction in it.

It's not just for gaining the ultimate buying commitment. This idea can be used at any stage in the sales process. You make a recommendation or suggestion, and you wrap it up with a statement such as "What do you think?" or "Does that seem logical to you?" or "Are you okay proceeding in this manner?" or any other question that keeps the process moving forward.

Says Alan Weiss in his book *Million Dollar Referrals*, "You're a peer of the buyer. Peers don't blatantly sell to one another. They recommend and suggest courses of action that can legitimately assist their peers. (Trust is the fervent belief that the other person has your sincere best interest in mind.)"

Internal-Sort Versus External-Sort

When it comes to buying something, sometimes we "internal-sort" the process, meaning we look inside ourselves for what feels right. We do our own research and come up with our own conclusions. Sometimes, we "external-sort" the process, meaning we want the help and advice of an expert. We seek that advice; we count on it. Depending on what we are buying, we may find ourselves sorting differently for different things.

Listen to what your prospects say and to what they ask. If you can see they are internally sorting, you say things like, "Here's something you might want to consider" and "What do you think the best solution would be for you?" If they are externally sorting, you want to be bolder with your recommendations (as stated above).

Are you making recommendations or suggestions to your prospects (or clients) about how to proceed to the next step? Or are you waiting for them to move the process forward? You can often move the process forward by making recommendations or suggestions!

CONFIRMING THE BUSINESS

Michael Vickers, author of *Becoming Preferred: How to Outsell Your Competition*, lays out his philosophy of "closing the sale." He writes, "If you have done your homework, asked all the right questions, taken the time to identify their needs, and gained a good understanding of their issues and key challenges, then the close is simply the next natural step in the process. If you have done it right, your prospective client will feel this way also.

"The most effective close that I know is simply this: after you have recapped, asked great questions and done your homework, and worked out several solutions that make sense, say, 'Based on all of the information you have given me and based on our discussions, these three solutions make the most sense to me. Which one makes the most sense to you?'"

Unfortunately, most salespeople and small business owners either don't seem to have much of a process or don't truly take care of the process. I know that I have been guilty of this over the years. When I have a clearly laid-out process—and follow it—I'm always more successful in confirming sales.

ACTION STEP

Get clear on your words, and practice until you feel extremely confident saying those words. Practice asking for the business!

APPENDIX 1

WHAT'S YOUR REFERRAL CONFIDENCE QUOTIENT?

Generating referrals is **not** rocket science. It really boils down to confidence. In the absence of confidence are fear, doubt, and inaction. Take this simple Referral Confidence Assessment to see where you stand on the confidence meter. Then, take this list and turn it into an action plan!

Rank your level of activity, confidence, or skill in each of the items below with a scale of:

- 1 = Not doing much here. Lack confidence
- 2 = Doing okay, but could boost level of activity and confidence.
- 3 = Doing quite well here. Could probably teach others.

	Referral-Generating Activity	1	2	3
1	I have fully committed—in actions and attitude—to building a referral-based business.			
2	I follow a specific process with all (or most) of my clients to make sure I provide maximum value early in the relationship.			
3	I have a well-defined client service model that keeps me on track in how I stay in touch with my clients and keeps my ongoing service at a high level—at least with my A clients.			
4	I have a written vision statement for my business, which I communicate clearly with my clients. All of my A and B clients know that I am open to taking on new clients who are the right fit.			
5	I am in the habit of promoting referrals (planting seeds for referrals) such as saying, "Don't keep me a secret!"			
6	I check in regularly with my clients to see where I stand with them, to fix problems, and to shed light on the value they have received.			
7	I have written out my script (or at least an outline) for asking for referrals and can ask for referrals clearly and succinctly.			
8	I ask for referrals on a regular basis.			
9	When a client doesn't want to talk about referrals, I have a confident and professional way to back out of the conversation (so the fear of "no" doesn't stop me from asking).			
10	When I get referrals, I learn as much as I can about the new prospects to qualify them for my business and to ensure a quality first conversation.			
11	I get the referral source involved in connecting (introducing) me to the new prospect.			

Referral-Generating Activity		1	2	3
12	I contact referral prospects quickly and keep the referral source in the loop.			
13	I send small thank you gifts to clients who give me referrals, not waiting for the prospect to become a client.			
14	I get my new referral clients to thank the referral source.			
15	I have created my "love list" of clients—clients who love me—and have asked them for referrals.			
16	I have identified the clients who have already given me referrals (even if I didn't ask) and have asked them for referrals.			
17	I have identified my A clients—the ones I want to clone—and have set up appointments with them to provide value and ask for referrals.			
18	I have a process for keeping track of new referral prospects so none of them fall through the cracks.			
19	I follow up with referral prospects in a professional way and have a system of staying in touch with continued value—until they become a client or they are clearly not interested in maintaining communication.			
20	I host client appreciation events to build business friendships, and I host referral events to meet new prospects in a social setting.			

How did you score?

50-60 points: You're a black belt in referrals!

40-49 points: You're a red belt—doing much better than average!

30-39 points: You're a white belt in referrals. You're engaged in the process, but you have a ways to go.

0-29 points: You're a pink belt in referrals. Otherwise what I call a Referral Wimp! Get some help! Read this book. *Read Get More Referrals Now!* Subscribe to my free e-mail newsletter: www.ReferralMinute.com

APPENDIX 2

PROFESSIONALS NEVER STOP PRACTICING

Just before I was about to deliver a keynote presentation for a large audience in Minneapolis, a small business owner came up to me and told me he was asking for referrals but was not having much success. I asked him to role-play with me for a minute. His request was choppy and wordy and lacked confidence. I asked him how many times he'd actually practiced asking for referrals. His answer was, "I guess that's something I need to do." Meaning he may never have practiced. Ever!

When I was a professional musician (yes, I toured the country as a drummer in a rock-and-roll band), I practiced two hours a day on my own and another two hours a day with the band, and then I played five to six hours, six nights per week.

Baseball players have off-season practice routines and spring training, and they take batting and fielding practice before every game. When do professional musicians and professional athletes stop practicing? When they retire! And some continue to practice even after retirement.

How often do you practice different aspects of your processes? Most people tend to wing it when they ask for referrals, call their new referral prospects, and run their sales appointments. This is a bad habit that surely leads to reduced sales effectiveness.

When you ask for referrals, make your sales calls, and run your sales appointments, the *first time* you say certain things or ask certain questions should not be in front of a prospect. When you wing it and try new ideas without a little practice, you tend to bumble and confuse things, use too many words to get to the point, and just plain lack confidence.

I run a Referral Champions Boot Camp twice a year. Attending one of my recent boot camps were two guys who were partners in a financial advisory practice. Per my recommendation, after the boot camp they set aside time to practice some of the things I taught, such as promoting referrals, asking for referrals, dealing with referral objections, and turning referrals into introductions. Once they gained some confidence, they took it to a higher level. They started running "pop quizzes" with each other. One would pop into the other's office and sit down and say, "Ask me for referrals." They did this at random times. The net result was that all these strategies became second nature to them. They truly mastered the referral process.

PRACTICE BREEDS CONFIDENCE

The process of asking for referrals, getting introductions, gaining appointments, and making sales is not rocket science. It's all about confidence. In the absence of confidence are fear, doubt, and certainly inaction. I think it was Jim Flowers who said, "Amateurs practice until they get it right. Professionals practice until they can't get it wrong!"

SOME IDEAS FOR MORE EFFECTIVE PRACTICE

Here are some real-life ideas I've gleaned from some of my clients over the last few years.

1. One professional uses a smartphone tripod on which he places his smartphone to record himself role-playing his request for referrals. He said he's tried it with a colleague, and he's even done this a few times by himself in the conference room. That

would be interesting to watch. Does he get up and run to the other side of the table to play each role?

2. A sales manager in Michigan has instituted biweekly "Pro Group" sessions. He says, "The concept is that pros practice. The key element of our execution is the practice effect. We video the role plays and review them during the session."

3. Another sales manager in Oklahoma runs quarterly full-day Referral Boot Camps. "Our reps showcase their process, and we do a ton of role play."

4. A sales manager in Maryland held a Referral Role-Play Tournament. This created a lot of practice and role-play competition. This resulted in a huge confidence boost for everyone, which translated into results.

5. A corporate client of mine—who uses one of our comprehensive video-training programs—holds referral practice sessions on a weekly basis. His sales team gathers together for about an hour each week to brainstorm on referrals. They share best practices, celebrate successes, work on questions and challenges, and almost always practice some aspect of the referral process. He told me that they usually video some of the role plays and that this recording can be extremely valuable. He said, "We had one guy who, every time he got nervous, would stick his finger in his ear. He had no idea he did this until he saw himself on video. Needless to say, this cured him of that bad habit."

My experience has taught me that it usually takes at least five to seven practice times before someone feels totally comfortable and effective asking for referrals and implementing any other part of the sales process. Unless you're the rare exception, you are probably not creating enough practice opportunities. Whether it's with referrals or anything else . . . Practice! Practice! Practice!

APPENDIX 3

GET YOUR ASSISTANT OR STAFF INVOLVED

The members of your staff can become involved in the referral process too. Perhaps they won't be asking for referrals like you, but they still have a role. Your staff should know what you're trying to accomplish with referrals and what their role is in that initiative.

First, your staff members play a crucial role in making you and your company more referable. They play a central role in the client experience. And even if they aren't in direct contact with clients, they are serving someone who is in direct contact. Every employee of a company contributes to the referability of that company.

Second, many of your staff can promote referrals with prospects and clients. Whenever they hear a client give an expression of value—such as "You guys did a great job for us"—then they can say things like, "Don't keep us a secret!" or "We're never too busy to see if we can provide the same value to others you care about."

Third, depending on the relationship you have with your assistant or other staff members, you can ask them to hold you accountable for asking for referrals. If you're a wimp when it comes to asking for referrals, tell a member of your staff, "I'm meeting with Sheri Thomas later today. She's extremely happy with our work. Ask me later if I asked her for referrals—like I should!" Now the fear of your assistant calling you a wimp can prompt you to face the lesser fear of asking for referrals.

SOME STAFF CAN ASK FOR REFERRALS

Some staff members are inclined and able to ask for referrals. For instance, Elizabeth is the marketing director for a financial advisor in Phoenix. Elizabeth knows that her advisor, Robert, has incredibly satisfied clients but will never bring himself to ask for referrals. So Elizabeth does it for him. She makes sure she gets to know the clients as best as she can. After they meet with Robert, she calls the clients to make sure they're happy. When they are, she asks for referrals and gets them.

Meet with the members of your staff to let them know how you want to incorporate referrals into the business. Consider giving them a copy of this book so they have more context for this discussion. Then, together, figure out what they can do (and are willing to do) to make your company more referable and more proactive for referrals.

INDEX

ABOUT THE AUTHOR

Bill Cates, CSP, CPAE, hails from Clarksville, Maryland, and is widely recognized as one of the foremost experts in the art and science of acquiring new clients through referrals and other relationship marketing strategies. His books, *Get More Referrals Now!* and *Don't Keep Me a Secret!* have revolutionized the way many business professionals are acquiring more and better clients through referrals. Bill is the president of Referral Coach International and the creator of *The Referral Advantage Program*™, *The Referral Champions System*™, and the *Unlimited Referrals System*™.

Inducted into the Professional Speakers Hall of Fame, Bill is a highly sought-after speaker on sales, marketing, and, of course, referrals. His referral system has been featured in such publications as *Success* magazine, *Entrepreneur* magazine, *Selling Power* and the *Wall Street Journal*. His own business success has been featured in *Money* magazine.

Bill is also somewhat of an adventurer. He has reached the summit of Mt. Kilimanjaro, trekked through the Himalayas, camped in the Arctic Circle, and toured the country as the drummer in a rock-and-roll band. His next adventure will be a visit to Antarctica in 2014.

www.ReferralCoach.com